DECISION MAKING&

SPIRITUAL DISCERNMENT

The Sacred Art of Finding Your Way

Nancy L. Bieber

Walking Together, Finding the Way ®
SKYLIGHT PATHS®
PUBLISHING
Nashville, Tennessee

Decision Making & Spiritual Discernment:
The Sacred Art of Finding Your Way

2016 Quality Paperback Edition

For information regarding permission to reprint material from this book, please mail or fax your request in writing to SkyLight Paths Publishing, Permissions Department, at the address / fax number listed below, or email your request to permissions@skylightpaths.com.

Grateful acknowledgment is given for permission to use material from the following sources: Unless otherwise stated, all biblical citations are from the *New Revised Standard Version Bible*, copyright © 1989, Division of Christian Education of the National Council of the Churches of Christ in the United States of America. Used by permission. All rights reserved. Pierre Teilhard de Chardin, "Patient Trust," translated by Michael Harter © The Institute of Jesuit Sources, St. Louis, Mo. All rights reserved. Used with permission. "Choosing Well, Living Whole" from *Facing East, Praying West: Poetic Reflections on the Spiritual Exercises*, by Kent Ira Groff, copyright © 2010 by Kent Ira Groff, Paulist Press, Inc., Mahwah, N.J. Reprinted by permission of Paulist Press, Inc. www.paulistpress.com. "It Felt Love" from *The Gift: Poems by Hafiz, the Great Sufi Master*, translated by Daniel Ladinsky. Published by Penguin Compass, copyright © 1999 by Daniel Ladinsky and used with his permission. Poem by Andrew Woff used by permission of the author. All the stories here based on individual experiences have been used with permission.

© 2010 by Nancy L. Bieber

Library of Congress Cataloging-in-Publication Data

Bieber, Nancy.
  Decision making & spiritual discernment : the sacred art of finding your way / Nancy L. Bieber. — Quality pbk. ed.
    p. cm.
  Includes bibliographical references (p.   ) and index.
  ISBN 978-1-59473-289-8 (quality pbk.)
  1. Decision making—Religious aspects. 2. Spiritual life. I. Title. II. Title: Decision making and spiritual discernment.
  BL629.5.D43B54 2010
  204'.4—dc22
                                                                    2010026772

ISBN 978-1-59473-333-8 (eBook)
Manufactured in the United States of America

Cover Design: Jenny Buono
Cover Photo: Larien G. Bieber
Interior Design: Kristi Menter

SkyLight Paths Publishing is creating a place where people of different spiritual traditions come together for challenge and inspiration, a place where we can help each other understand the mystery that lies at the heart of our existence.

SkyLight Paths sees both believers and seekers as a community that increasingly transcends traditional boundaries of religion and denomination—people wanting to learn from each other, *walking together, finding the way.*

SkyLight Paths, "Walking Together, Finding the Way," and colophon are trademarks of LongHill Partners, Inc., registered in the U.S. Patent and Trademark Office.

Walking Together, Finding the Way®·
Published by SkyLight Paths Publishing
An Imprint of Turner Publishing Company
4507 Charlotte Avenue, Suite 100
Nashville, TN 37209
Tel: (615) 255-2665
www.skylightpaths.com

CONTENTS

MAKING A START

Every November my family gathers for a three-day-long reunion. From all over the country, we stream into a big cabin in the woods, all of us from the family patriarch to the youngest great-grandchild. We crowd into a large room with a fireplace, and, piling coats in the corners, greet each other with hugs and cries of delight. Games, food, books, babies, and visiting fill our days. One morning last year we sat around in a circle for a grand sharing time, telling each other of the struggles and celebrations of the year. This was our special opportunity for listening, and I listened with laughter and with tears to the stories of these people I love. What amazed me most was how much change everyone was facing. Some were choosing change, while others had it thrust upon them. But all of us were experiencing change within our lives.

Around the room, major life transitions were emerging like flowers in April. Almost everyone was moving, getting jobs, losing jobs, having babies, starting school or finishing school, taking on a responsibility or letting it go. Some were learning how to face and grapple with what they didn't choose: the loss of a spouse, diminishment of health or finances. Others were choosing change (a new house) or learning how to live with the decisions they had made (a new baby). We were confused and hopeful and scared and trusting as we sat around on couches or cushions on the floor, listening to each other while we entertained the toddlers who wandered around.

The recent college graduate reported that a couple of months ago, he felt he had as much light for his future as was provided by a flickering match. Now, he said, it was still dark but he thought he had a flashlight in his hand. A young married couple knew the direction in which they wanted to go, but the details of how to step forward into their future were still foggy. He wanted to find a new approach to teaching music, while she was drawn to both teaching and counseling. One sister was rebuilding her life after her husband's death and another sister was rebuilding hers in a new state with a new job.

Then it was my turn. I spoke about feeling restless, about sensing that I was ready for something new, but not knowing what it might be. "Last summer," I told my family, "I decided it was time to practice what I preached. I decided to do a spiritual discernment practice that I've often taught to others but never used for myself."

This is the practice I used: Imagine that you are on your deathbed or are very elderly and infirm. You know you don't have a long time to live. You are reflecting on your life, looking back over its chapters. Ask yourself this question: *What is there that you regret never having done?*

When I posed that question to myself, an immediate answer flashed before me: *Write!* Well, of course, I thought. I knew that already. Writing has always called to me, but usually I've ignored the call. Except for a few articles, I hadn't honored this persistent nagging voice. As I hesitated, wondering whether this was the time to honor that voice, it grew louder: *You're in your sixties, you know. You don't have forever. If not now, when?*

"But I don't know anything about writing something substantial," I protested to the voice. "I don't know publishing. What if I can't do it?" At that point I seemed to hear the thunderous voice of my old friend Jonathan: "Get out there and *fail,* Nancy. Just get out there." And so I began. Although I had no idea where I was going, I acknowledged that this was the time. I gave a firm "yes" to that persistent inner voice.

"Then," I told my family at the reunion, "the miracle happened." Exactly one month later I received a phone call from a woman I'd never heard of. She told me she was an editor and had tracked me down to ask if I'd ever considered writing a book on spiritual discernment. She'd seen the publicity for retreats I had led on spiritual discernment and thought there was value in expanding the material into a book. I told the others, "It took me days to recover from the shock of that call. Would-be writers just don't receive those kinds of phone calls—especially just after deciding to be a writer!"

But I gave a definitive "yes" to the editor, my second "yes" to writing. It seemed as if I had no choice. The inner voice that insisted I write was the Spirit nudging me, even though it felt more like a shove off the edge of a cliff. I was going on an adventure. I invite you to join me on that adventure as we explore spiritual discernment and learn to find our way through the multitude of decisions in our lives.

MAKING DECISIONS AND SPIRITUAL DISCERNMENT

At the family reunion, the stories we heard covered a wide range of decisions. Actually, it was not an unusual gathering. Change is constant; we are always making choices or responding to events in our lives. Making decisions is part of life. Some decisions are challenging; our very survival seems to hang in the balance. The right job hasn't been offered despite lots of applications, but the bills are piling up, so you are forced to take what you can find. Or, say, you are living with a verbally abusive spouse. Must you leave and risk life alone in order to survive? Faced with such survival decisions, what should you do?

Other decisions might be called fulfillment decisions. You decide to pay attention to a dream, to follow it and see where it leads. Or perhaps a general unhappiness with the shape of your days leads you to reevaluate what's really important and what you want your life to be about. You know there is more to living than the pattern you're stuck in, and you decide to do something about it.

Still other decisions turn out to be mistakes. They have unforeseen consequences, and you have to decide how to live with them if you can't change them. Oftentimes, the decisions you have to make are about responding to something you didn't choose at all. A death, a divorce, or the loss of a job uproots you against your will. You have to learn how to live with something that is hard to live with, something you never intended to happen. Stumbling, you make decisions both large and small as you find the way through difficult events like these.

When we make a decision, even a small one, it expresses something about our fundamental values. We make decisions according to what gives meaning and worth to our lives. Our decisions reflect what we treasure most. Today I have only made small decisions. I had to choose whether to serve on a committee, go for a hike under a rain-threatening sky, and whether to spend the extra money to buy organic and local. While checking e-mail, I decided to add my name to a political petition and I turned down an opportunity to buy more camping gear. If someone charted my small daily decisions—how I use my time and how I spend my money—they'd find that they express my values as much as the really big life decisions do. Everyday decisions come in clusters. Like pins clinging to a magnet, our small daily choices cling loyally to the central values of our lives.

We all want to make *good* decisions, ones that will shape our lives well. We want to make our choices carefully and wisely. If we're honest with ourselves, we know we could use some help in clearly seeing the way to go and understanding all the complexities of our decision making. We need something to help us step forward.

This book presents a spiritual process for wise decision making and for beginning to live out the decisions we've made. It is the process of spiritual discernment.

Making decisions is inherently sacred work, even when we don't recognize it as such. Through our decisions, we shape our unique and sacred lives. And whether the decision is large and life-altering or of the small daily variety, it will flow more smoothly when we recognize it as a sacred process, and are willing to allow the Spirit to illuminate our decision making.

To make wise decisions, we need the aid of that wise and loving Spirit whose wisdom and light exceed our own. With the Spirit illuminating the complexities of our decisions, we can see and understand more about ourselves and our choices. *Spiritual discernment* is the process of opening our lives and decisions to God and being attentive to what we see with the aid of the divine Light.

When we open all our decisions to the Spirit, we learn to see more clearly what is true and real. We explore opportunities, and are better able to distinguish between those that are right for us and those that aren't. In *Listening Spirituality: Personal Spiritual Practices Among Friends,* Patricia Loring compares discernment to developing an "ear" for music or an "eye" for the arts. As we practice discernment, we grow more skilled at discerning which choices are in harmony with God's ways, and we create our unique way forward with God.

Sometimes people understand "God's will" or "God's plan" as something imposed on us by God, something we must discover and decipher. I understand it differently. I feel that God's path for our lives is constantly being developed. It rises within us and is something we develop in partnership with God as we learn to see and understand more clearly. With this seeing and understanding, we find the courage to step into the future.

The foundation of spiritual decision making and spiritual discernment is opening to God. We acknowledge gladly that we are not depending entirely on our own abilities to think and compare, to feel and envision. We want the light and wisdom of God to shine out and influence our thought process and analytical reasoning, our feelings and hopes. We recognize that this is the way to good decisions.

THE THREE STRANDS OF SPIRITUAL DISCERNMENT

When I was a child growing up on a farm, I wore my hair in pigtails. I learned to braid them myself, holding the three strands and folding each in turn into the center to create a long, smooth braid strong enough to withstand the tumbles of an active country girl.

A braid of three strands, woven securely together, describes the plan for this book as well. There are three parts, each focusing on a central theme of spiritual discernment. Even though I've separated the strands to write about them, the truth is that they are woven together as we live. In spiritual discernment, as in braiding, each strand takes its turn; none can be ignored if we are to learn and practice a strong decision making process.

The three strands or themes that we will braid together are *willingness, attentiveness,* and *responsiveness.* Through many years as a clinical psychologist, and as a spiritual director and teacher, I have listened to and counseled hundreds of people facing life changes and trying to make wise decisions. As I have journeyed with them through change and decision making, I have found that willingness, attentiveness, and responsiveness weave together again and again, creating a strong rope to grasp on to, a clear practice for making life decisions.

Willingness is the focus of Part I. Being willing to open ourselves to the Spirit's light and wisdom acknowledges our limited ability to make good decisions on our own. It means we are willing to receive, actually expecting to receive, loving guidance. An attitude of willingness is a combination of "Help!" and "Yes." It's an approach to God that admits that we are in too deep, even if we're only "in" a couple of inches. We need a guiding hand and a brighter light to find the way that is right.

It might be tempting to quickly scan through this section of the book, moving on to the later sections, where it seems we're really doing something. However, I urge you to take time for willingness. Because we usually like to be in control of our lives, acknowledging that there may be a divine Light greater than our own insight can be hard. Being willing means we release our tight control and engage with God to discover the best way forward. This is fundamental to spiritual discernment.

In Part II we turn to *attentiveness*. Being attentive to what is true and real is at the heart of spiritual decision making. We pause and consider carefully who we are, who we dream of being, and the life situations in which we find ourselves. We discover what we already know, though we often didn't know we knew it. We discover mysterious yearnings and see them more clearly in the divine Light. We often find ourselves filled with contradictions and confusion because we are enormously complicated beings.

The word *discernment* is about paying attention, about noticing those fine differences that are complicated and hard to distinguish. It's not the black-and-white decisions, but the gray choices to which we have to pay attention. Like my husband sorting his socks (black and very dark blue), we need all the light we can get to study the colors of our possible choices. He waits for morning sunlight to stream into the room. We lean on God's illumination.

Responsiveness is the third theme in the interwoven braid. In Part III we respond to what we've been attentive to, what we've learned through God's illumination of ourselves and our situation. It may seem as if we're *finally* doing something, making a decision, taking some steps, getting somewhere. This may be the most visible part of spiritual decision making, but it's not the end point. It simply continues the process of creating with God. We continually renew our willing openness to the Light and pay attention to the landscape within and around us.

Responding is like conducting a complex experiment. Even when we've been attentive and thoughtful, we don't know for sure how it will turn out. We sort through and take stock of what we know. We consider what the next step might be, and we learn from both the paths that are open to us and those that are closed. Sometimes our responding is simply waiting, but waiting attentively for what is to come next.

Willingness, attentiveness, and *responsiveness* are the three themes we braid together. Like the strands of a braid, each depends on the others in the movement of weaving. We may move from attentiveness to willingness and on to responding by taking a step, and then renew our attentiveness without realizing how we're braiding them all together. It is a blessed dance.

As a child, I sometimes braided my hair unevenly, and one strand didn't have enough hairs gathered together to do its part. Likewise, we may skimp on one of these three aspects of spiritual decision making. We might be open to God's guidance but never respond by taking any steps. We could be so eager for a change that we aren't attentive to the Light and its wisdom. All three aspects of this process are essential for wise decisions to be made and lived out.

GOD AT THE CENTER

Although God is at the center of our decision making, we all come with unique understandings about God. Some of us have a religious tradition with well-established names and qualities for the Divine, while others may claim no religious tradition at all and simply have a basic belief in the Spirit and the importance of the spiritual aspect of life.

There are many names for God around the world, all of them attempts to describe something that is larger than any names. They all reflect our understandings of the Spirit. I have my favorite names; you probably have yours. Mine include Spirit, Love, Guide, and Light, among other names that I use in this book. One of my favorite names for God is the one I learned from author and teacher Tilden Edwards: Something More. It reminds me that God is always more, more than our names, more vast and more intimate than we can understand.

Perhaps the God name that is most helpful for spiritual discernment is Light. When we have to make decisions, to find our way, we need all the illumination we can get. God is a Light that brings clarity into our dark confusion and helps us see the way. The image of lifting ourselves and our quandary into a Light that helps us see and understand more clearly is found in many religious traditions. The Qur'an describes Allah as the "light of heavens and earth," while Hindu writings refer to Brahman as the "light of lights." Christianity sees that "God is light and in him there is no darkness at all." My Quaker tradition uses light as a metaphor for the transcendent God and describes that which is of God within us as the inner light.

GETTING STARTED: HOW TO USE THIS BOOK

The three sections I have outlined, *Willingness, Attentiveness,* and *Responsiveness,* describe the process of spiritual decision making, and also provide an order for traveling through it. Each chapter provides its own important step in this process. We interweave the steps as we go deeper into the process, returning to being willing and attentive even as we are responding.

If you are actively working on making a decision, read each chapter as it comes and do practices at the end of it. Some chapters and practices may meet your needs more than others. Spend as much time as you can with the practices that seem right for you. Even if you are not part of a group, you may find it helpful to answer the questions contained in the "Guide for Groups" in the appendix.

As you move from chapter to chapter, you may find yourself making a decision at any time. The needed clarity for the decision you're working on might come at any point. We often make big decisions in stages, each pace forward a necessary step along the way.

If you are *not* actively working on a major decision, the book can be a guide to deeper spiritual living in daily life. Explore practices that will help you know yourself better (chapters 3 and 4, in particular). Or perhaps you will be drawn to deepen your openness to the Spirit (all chapters, but particularly chapters 1, 2, and 5) or strengthen your attentiveness in daily life (particularly chapter 6). Find the sections that speak to you most and spend time with them.

THE PRACTICES

At the end of each chapter, detailed spiritual practices or exercises invite you to apply the chapter's focus to your own life in a very practical way. This is the opportunity to truly "work" the book. Whether you are facing a major decision or simply want better tools for making decisions, the end-of-chapter practices are valuable aids. Reading the book through without engaging in at least some of the practices is like looking at a beautiful landscape just outside your window, but never stepping outside. You're missing the opportunity to learn more about who you are and who you can become.

I urge you to keep a notebook or journal specifically to write down what you've learned from the book, especially from the practices. Some practices require listing, naming, or remembering something of importance. Having all your insights together in one place is a valuable resource for the future.

GROUP STUDY

In order to use *Decision Making and Spiritual Discernment* in group sessions, I have provided a guide for a series of six group sessions at the end of this book. Your religious community or perhaps a small group of committed friends may find that reading and experiencing the practices together helps support their individual decision-making journeys and strengthens their sense of the Spirit's presence and activity in their lives.

As the author, I deeply hope that *Decision Making and Spiritual Discernment* will grow shabby with use. I hope that it will be marked up and have turned-down corners, signs of its service to you. And I hope you return to it repeatedly through the years so that it will again and again give you encouragement and direction as you make decisions.

~⌐

ABBREVIATIONS

Unless otherwise stated, all biblical citations are from the *New Revised Standard Version Bible*. The following abbreviations for biblical translations are used in the text:

KJV = King James Version

NIV = New International Version

NRSV = New Revised Standard Version

Here we are, Loving One, Mystery, Light,
beginning to quiet ourselves,
beginning to be still;

remembering you created us
to flourish in your love,
remembering an old desire to grow in you.

We long to be more than we are living now,
we long to live all we can become
but, fearful, wonder how we can.

We try to choose the best and truest path
but stumble in our living and in our choosing.
We want to handle things ourselves;
we'd rather make it on our own,
and besides,
trusting you, God, can be very hard.

But we need more light, your Light
to see the ways ahead,
we need more wisdom, yours, to choose
the way that's well for us.

Here we are, beginning willingness,
beginning to trust, to open ourselves,
our lives and our decisions
to your illuminating Light.

Here we are, Loving One, ready to begin.

PART I

WILLINGNESS

OPENING WITH A "YES"

IT FELT LOVE
How
Did the rose
Ever open its heart

And give to this world
All its
Beauty?

It felt the encouragement of light
Against its
Being,

Otherwise,
We all remain

Too

Frightened.

—Hafiz

I've often watched with fascination as my flowers open and reach for the light. I love to garden, but I'm the kind of gardener who sometimes doesn't get around to staking the salvia, the tall gladiolus stalks, or the big burnt-orange marigolds. Just when they should be spectacularly blooming, they flop over, bowed down by a rainy wind or by the heaviness of their blossoms. A couple of days later, when I finally come with stakes to prop them up, I find they have already made their own correction; their tips have bent to grow straight up again. They've done a ninety-degree turn to raise their blossoming heads. Built into their nature, their genetic code, is a reach toward light.

Like the flowers in my garden, like the rose in the poem we have just read by the fourteenth-century Sufi poet Hafiz, you and I have been created to reach toward the light and to bloom. We are designed to open, created to bloom. And there is light: A loving God is continually inviting us to open. Hafiz translator Daniel Ladinsky titled the poem "It Felt Love," though he used the word *light* in the poem itself. Light and Love are both names for God, and we are designed to respond to them in their many forms. When my small granddaughters stretch out their arms to be picked up, they are reaching for love. A teacher once told me that a note of appreciation she received made her feel as if she were "dancing in sunlight." Love brings a glow to the face and energy to the dance of daily life.

However, unlike the flower in sunlight, we could be "too frightened" to open. We could stretch to release into the world more beauty than we knew we contained, or we might remain tightly furled in fear and resistance. Experiences of brokenness and pain from childhood traumas or adult insecurities can frighten us into remaining closed. Fear prevents our human blooming more than the shade of a spreading maple tree prevents the sun-seeking rosebush from blooming. In the next chapter we'll look at fears that hamper our response, but first we'll address our yearning to fulfill our true nature and open in the Light.

MUTUAL YEARNING

Last summer Andy went camping with friends. Late at night, when everyone else was sleeping, he was still wakeful. Sitting by the edge of the small lake, listening to the quiet sounds of water and a breeze rustling in the trees, he thought over the last year. His father, with whom he shared a business, had died unexpectedly, leaving him to sort out tangled business affairs, support his grieving mother, and deal with his own grief. He'd been struggling for months, trying to straighten out the business and discover, as he said, "who I am now." He looked up into the brilliance of the stars and suddenly felt that there was a vast presence around, something more than he could name. Andy says he's not a particularly religious person, but he felt as if there was something big going on, and somehow he was in it or part of it. And he knew that he *wanted* to be part of it. He sat there for a long time feeling more peace than he'd felt for a long time, knowing he was not alone and that he could trust the unfolding of this new stage of his life.

The first decision in this book on decision making is to allow ourselves to open to God, to trust our yearning for God. Can we sit there, as Andy did, and open to it? It helps when we know God is yearning for us, too. It reminds us that the sun's *encouragement* of the rose is a metaphor for God's reaching out to us. Like the rose, we are invited to respond to something that is already happening: Love's gentle encouragement. God is a love that pours itself out, longing for us to open and become the particular flower we were created to become. We're invited to become part of a grand, sustainable love project. Together we can create the beauty that is our deepest selves.

Even when we get hurt or scared and close up, pulling our petals into tightly sealed buds again, God's loving reach still comes, more constant than the sun. Nothing changes God's love, which continues to pour into us and invite us to open. Even if we think we're sealed up tight, there's almost always a tiny opening somewhere where Light can enter. We can still be stirred by the mysterious invitation of Love and may, almost imperceptibly at first, begin to respond.

God also invites us to be open to a wisdom greater than our own, a wisdom that helps us discern which choices are the right ones for the unique situation we're facing, which choices will stretch us to bloom in the way we were designed to bloom. Being attentive to God's wisdom helps us discern which paths will draw us closer to God and God's loving ways and which will not.

However, our human reaching for God is often hidden from ourselves, disguised as a vague dissatisfaction or a yearning for something other than God. We humans often want something, yet we might not know what it is we truly want. Maybe we think we want love or happiness or maybe we just feel unsettled and dissatisfied with the pattern of our days. Life's not dreadful, but it could be better. Oftentimes, this discomfort rumbles around in the background of our lives, creating a restless discontent. Like a distant thunderstorm, it never brings the downpour of rain that would clear the atmosphere, but it doesn't go away, either. We can expend considerable energy, time, and money distracting ourselves from this discontent or trying to satisfy the yearning for something more.

When the fourth-century church leader Augustine of Hippo wrote his *Confessions,* he prayed, "God, you have formed us for yourself, and our hearts are restless till they find rest in you." Augustine knew about restlessness. His young adult years were all about seeking and not finding what he wanted. He led a life of pleasure, he had lovers, he tried on the various philosophies of his age, but nothing worked for long. It wasn't until he was in his thirties that he heard God calling through the voice of a child singing in a garden. Following that call, he returned to Africa from Rome and gave his life to strengthening the Christian community there.

This restless state has been described as a God-shaped vacuum within us that only God can fill. The power of the vacuum lies in its urgent need to be filled. It is amazingly easy to pour into it all kinds of things. Into the vacuum we sometimes pour activities whose basic purpose is to keep us busy. We throw in all those things that advertisers promise will bring us love and fulfill-ment—the new car, new clothes, the newest electronic equip-ment. Yet they simply don't fill the unique God space in us.

As the prophet Isaiah said to the people of Israel when they were exiled in a strange land:

> Ho, everyone who thirsts,
> come to the waters;
> and you that have no money,
> come, buy and eat!
> Come, buy wine and milk
> without money and without price.
> Why do you spend your money for that which is not bread,
> and your labor for that which does not satisfy?
> Listen carefully to me, and eat what is good,
> and delight yourselves in rich food.
>
> —Isaiah 55:1–2

Isaiah throws out a challenge for us in our own day. We need to open ourselves to what is life-giving, say "yes" to "what is good," and then "listen carefully" so that we may live. Our human need to receive love into our lives and to fulfill the potential we *know* we have within us can be as urgent as the vacuum's need to fill itself. Our challenge is to open to God so that we may find the paths and make the decisions that will be life-giving.

SAYING "YES"

Dag Hammarskjold, the Swedish diplomat who became United Nations secretary-general, wrote in *Markings,* the story of his spiritual journey:

> I don't know Who or—what—put the question, I don't know when it was put. I don't even remember answering.

But at some moment I did answer *Yes* to Someone—
or Something—and from that hour I was certain that
existence is meaningful and that, therefore, my life, in
self-surrender, had a goal.

At some moment, we too need to choose "yes." Answering "yes"
is our way of opening in the Light. It is unfurling our petals and
giving to the world more of whom we are created to be. Yes, I
will acknowledge that I need the Spirit to help steer my living.
Yes, I need love and meaning for my life; I need to experience
being filled, to quiet my restless, seeking heart. I need to find my
way home. Yes, I am willing.

For Dag Hammarskjold, saying "yes" was returning to the
"Someone" or "Something" that gave his life meaning. It was
saying "yes" to a way of living, a self-surrender that brought
purpose into his work. With the "yes," he traveled the world as
a peacemaker and negotiator, a United Nations advocate working for the common good. For us, like Dag Hammarskjold, saying "yes" is the first step in the journey of spiritual discernment
and decision making. Our "yes" is the expression of our willingness. With our "yes" we make the commitment to live, to shape
our decisions, and to discern the way forward with the Spirit's
help.

If we were to listen closely for the Spirit's response to our
"yes," we might hear words like these:

Of course. I created you to seek and to find Me. You are
responding out of your truest nature. I will fill the vacuum
that troubles you. I am the Light that will illuminate your
way. I have been longing for you to reach toward me. Let
us join together and create the path.

In spite of that welcoming voice, we often struggle for years with
that "yes," especially if we've been caught up in an endless cycle

of trying to fill the vacuum in destructive ways. Writer Anne Lamott bluntly describes her efforts to find something—any-thing—that could fill the emptiness. From her early teens, she used drugs and alcohol, and she binged on food. Yet even at her most desperate, she felt God's pull, and she yearned for some-thing more. In some of her books she recounts the journey of her small "yes" steps and how they mixed with her resistance. In *Traveling Mercies,* she describes her journey as "a series of stag-gers" and a "lurch" rather than a leap of faith.

Though she longed for something more, Lamott was caught up in what psychiatrist and spiritual director Gerald May calls willfulness. In his book *Will and Spirit,* May describes the differ-ence between willingness and willfulness. Willingness is "saying yes to the mystery of being alive in each moment" while willful-ness is "saying no, or perhaps more commonly, 'Yes, but' ..." Like Anne Lamott, we all tend toward willfulness sometimes, even though it keeps us stuck in trying to figure everything out by ourselves, depending only on ourselves to find our way as best we can. Willingness, saying "yes," frees us to consider more pos-sibilities than we knew and invites God's wisdom to help us sort them out.

SETTING WILLINGNESS IN MOTION

There is something mysterious about saying "yes." It sets things in motion. Whether it is to a marriage proposal, a job offer, or an invitation to get together with friends, something shifts when we say "yes." Something is beginning. In the first minute or two, nothing actually looks different. We haven't entered the mar-riage, started the job, gone to the party. We have, however, opened to a specific yet unknown future. Whether that seems more like a risk or a great delight, the fact that we've said "yes" to it changes things.

Our "yes" to God profoundly changes us, too. Something shifts within us when we choose to say "yes." We are beginning a specific yet unknown journey into greater harmony with divine music. Thomas Merton, the Trappist monk, wrote, "Our real journey in life is interior; it is a matter of growth, deepening, and of an even greater surrender to the creative action of love and grace in our hearts." The creative force of love and grace is always present and inviting us to venture deeper spiritually. By assenting to this creative force, we release its power to mysteriously begin to work within us.

Many years ago, I met with a woman who was struggling vocationally. To support herself and her family, she needed to work full-time at a retail job with lots of stress and low pay, but she longed to become a minister. When she spoke to her pastor, he encouraged her to see her present work as a place she was called to. But she couldn't accept that. At one point in our conversation, she blurted out, "God doesn't waste willingness."

I don't know where her journey has taken her now, but I do know that she spoke truth. Whether her willingness took her to seminary, helped her become the unofficial chaplain of the local Sears or Penney's, bringing a loving and compassionate presence into a challenging environment, or perhaps opened her to some completely unexpected ministry, God did not waste her willingness.

Being open and willing involves all of ourselves—our minds, our hearts, and our bodies. Because the thinking self specializes in reason, considering causes and effects, planning and analyzing, the mind's "yes" to God's invitation quickly turns practical: How do I do that? What are the steps to take? Are there problems to solve here? These are important questions to ask. But saying "yes" is opening to wisdom beyond the mind's own. This willingness seems to access the kind of knowing we call intuitive.

The reasoning mind's analytical ability needs to open to God's wisdom so it can honor the more subtle knowing of intuitive wisdom. I treasure my ability to solve problems, and I believe God's guidance for my life comes through all my thinking faculties—both intuitive and reasoning. However, I often trust my rational knowing more than my intuitive knowing. I need to turn to God's wisdom, which flows through all kinds of knowing and helps me open to the full life I want to live.

The heart's experience of "yes" lies in the feelings we have when we open to God. We have ached for connection to something more. Our hearts have known the restlessness Augustine wrote about. So our heart's "yes" comes with feelings of gladness and joy. There can be a deep relief at having something besides ourselves to help us find our way through the confusing decisions and conflicting choices of daily life. Embracing that is liberating and freeing.

It may also feel risky. Trusting another, even God, can make us feel vulnerable. Even when we consider ourselves co-creators with God, we might be worried about the One we're collaborating with. So fear can be present in our heart's "yes," because it is sometimes hard to remember that God is inherently trustworthy. Heart and mind may be in conflict: The heart feels willing to acknowledge its need for Love so we can open and bloom, but the mind resists the idea. Or the mind knows there is a greater wisdom that will help illuminate the path, but the heart doesn't feel comfortable with that much vulnerability. Sometimes we may say "yes" when we're not wholly willing.

That is why using the body is so important. Saying "yes" with our bodies can affirm and unite the heart's and the mind's willingness to open to God. When we are willing, when we are trusting, we tend to open our hands, extend them forward, raise them toward the heavens. By contrast, when we close down, our hands clench, our arms cross tightly on the chest, our backs are rigidly upright. When inviting God in, we might bow our heads or kneel in the ancient traditional posture of acceptance and acknowledgment of allegiance to One who is greater. If we're Muslim, we will kneel on the floor with arms outstretched, a posture of submission and acceptance of the greatness of Allah.

Bodily posture never guarantees that the whole self is joining in. Opening to God is an inner experience, a willingness that shifts something inside us. But when the inner experience happens, the outer expression confirms and strengthens it.

When my husband and I are traveling and trying to decide which road to take, we discuss it together. Sometimes I say "yes" to his preference for unpaved roads that wind up into the hills, knowing it will become an adventure. However, my "yes" must come from my whole self. An inner "I don't really want to" combined with an outer "yes" spells disaster. It must be a heartfelt "Yes, let's do it!" or we both lose.

"Yes, let's do it!" opens us to an adventurous God journey, but only when head and heart are both willing. Our willingness to be guided by illumination from the Spirit in creating our life path is the key to the adventure. When we make our decisions with the Creator—the small, daily ones as well as the major life-direction choices—we're on to the big adventure.

RETURNING TO "YES" AGAIN—AND AGAIN

Catholic priest and author Henri Nouwen wrote in *The Inner Voice of Love* that God says to us, "I love you, I am with you, I want to see you come closer to me and experience the joy and peace of my presence.... Just trust me and let me be your God." Then he adds, "This is the voice to listen to. And that listening requires a real choice, not just once in a while but every moment of each day and night." Nouwen means that we need to choose to trust God as our Guide over and over again. We need to say "yes" again and again.

Imagine that you are an instrument in God's grand orchestra. As the orchestra tunes up, the concertmaster signals the oboe to play an A note and all the instruments are tuned to that note. But they need to be tuned repeatedly because over time they will inevitably drift slightly out of harmony with the oboe's A. In God's orchestra, our willingness, our "yes," tunes us to play in harmony with God's A note. Naturally, we drift away from it over time. Our return to willingness, our choice to trust God, brings us back again and again.

In the Introduction, I told the story of how I came to write this book. I wrote of my trepidation and of my great amazement at the Spirit's encouragement. As I continued exploring this project and taking the steps to develop it, I needed to remain open to the Spirit's leading. Yet as time went on and I planned the structure I'd use, wrote an introduction, and waited for acceptance from the publisher, it began to seem like *my* project. I thought it was totally up to me to succeed in finding the words to describe spiritual discernment. It was totally up to me to write efficiently so I'd meet the deadline I'd agreed to. Friends told me I'd do a great job, and I began to think I needed to meet their expectations. Those expectations began to feel like a burden.

One day I was walking along a country road near my home when I suddenly realized that I'd forgotten to listen to the Guide who shared the work, the Guide whose work I wanted to write about! When I found myself in that quandary, the only way through it was to remember my yearning for God. I needed to reaffirm my openness to God's guidance, to say "yes" again.

As I continued to walk, I rediscovered my willingness. My prayer became, "God, this is *your* project. I am yours. I am working with you on this writing. I release it to you." I opened my hands, signifying assent. I came again to a heartfelt and mindful willingness, a "yes" that freed me to continue writing line by line, discerning my way step by step, and trusting the outcome to One who can see further than I can. I'd love to be able to say that I stayed in that calm frame of mind, that I remembered to choose to be open to the Spirit whose wisdom about making decisions is so much more than my own. But I forgot again and again. I became anxious repeatedly. I needed to choose to say "yes," to return to my willingness again and again.

Because we are human, we lose touch with willingness again and again. This provides us with the opportunity to return to "yes" again and again. The mystery of willingness is that we do return, and the presence of the Spirit continues to fulfill our longing, guide our deciding, and enlarge our loving.

As one of the three themes in our spiritual discernment and decision making, *willingness* weaves through all our discernment. It is in our *attentiveness* as we listen more deeply for what is really true about our lives and become awake to divine nudges. It's in our *responsiveness*. It gives us courage to take steps, to explore options, and to gather the patience to wait when we need to.

Willingness begins the journey that, like Hafiz's rose, brings forth the beauty for which we have been created. Wherever we are, the beauty with which we have been created glows more brightly when we are open to the Light. Opening to God shapes our living in ways that remain mysterious even as we rejoice in their rightness.

Practices for Finding Your Way

Through the practices that follow, you can find many ways to express your willingness. Perhaps you will open to God and quiet your restless spirit. Perhaps you will let go of the belief that you are the chief manager of your life. Or you may find Light's encouragement is warming you into blooming.

THE BODY'S WILLINGNESS

This practice invites your body to join in your willingness to open. Sit or stand—whichever seems right for you.

1. Begin with a deep breath, taking in and releasing it so your whole body is aware of your breath and you

know you are in your body. Then, breathing easily and naturally, notice your body. Be attentive to your head, your arms and hands, your legs and feet, the trunk of your body and how your chest lifts and drops slightly with each breath. Be aware of your blood and your nerves spreading throughout your body from your skull to your toes.

2. When you have "rediscovered" your body, invite it to express its willingness to open to God. How will your body join in your "yes"? You may bow your head, or raise your arms and head upward. You may kneel or prostrate yourself. You may jump up and down, with an excited, eager "yes, yes!" Perhaps, as you are sitting, your palms gently unfold.

3. Hold the posture for a little while and feel your willingness deepen within you.

WELCOMING THE LIGHT

This practice acknowledges your willingness to be open to God and welcomes the Light for your journey of discernment. It joins words and movement. You may sit or stand—whichever feels right for you.

1. Find words that express your opening to and welcoming of God as Light to illuminate your way. You may say something like "I welcome the Light into my being" or "God, I welcome you as the Light that guides me." If you are a Christian, you may open and welcome the light of Christ to illuminate your way. Repeat the words slowly and carefully. You may imagine it like sunlight pouring down on you or shining within you as you speak.

2. Using your arms or hands, make a gesture of welcome. How do you greet a dear friend coming into your home? Let your welcome express that gladness.

3. Repeat this exercise by welcoming the Light into your mind and thinking, into your heart and feeling, into your life energy. Welcome it into your seeing and your hearing, into any area of you that needs it. Give yourself time to be with each gesture and expression of welcome so you can more deeply feel it. You might touch your head as you welcome the Light into your mind, or touch your heart, eyes, and ears as you name them.

THE ROSE: A VISUAL MEDITATION

This practice invites you to imagine you are Hafiz's rose, ready to bloom. You may want to return to this meditation many times, especially when you need to remember that you are created to bloom.

1. Sit comfortably with your eyes closed. Settle yourself by focusing on your breathing for a few minutes. Picture yourself as an unopened rosebud. Know what color you are and what kind of rose you are (shrub, climber, miniature, antique rose?). Picture yourself planted in an open area with your roots deep in the soil.

2. Imagine that it is very early morning, and light is just beginning to show in the east. Though night's chill lingers, the light brings a subtle eagerness into your flower self. You know that this day you will open and bloom.

3. Imagine the sun's rays falling upon you, warming your petals. Imagine the gentle opening of your outer petals and then the slow unwrapping of the layers of inner petals. Know that you have a lovely rose scent that perfumes the warm air around you. Experience delight in your own beauty, gladness in the relaxing of your petals, and gratitude for the sun.

WRITING A LETTER TO GOD

This practice is particularly helpful to those of us who need words to understand what we are feeling.

1. As you begin to write, use the name for God that fits your understanding best. Think through what names are right for you at this time, recognizing that they may change even in the course of your letter.

2. Write in this letter whatever you wish to say to God. Include somewhere in it a sentence or paragraph describing the state of your openness and willingness. If you are not feeling open, write that. If you feel an unsatisfied longing, write it out. If you can express gladness about God's involvement in your life, express that. You may find that you become more open to God as you write.

3. You may conclude with an expression of how you would like to be known by God. What name is yours? How do you wish to sign off? Perhaps it is a quality (Joy or Stubborn One or Thirsty One) or a name descriptive of the relationship you have or the one you would like to have (Child or God Dancer), or simply your given name.

YES TO THE HEAVENS

This is a very simple practice of being outdoors in the natural world. You can sit, stand, or move actively in the outdoor space.

1. Choose an outdoor spot that reveals the beauty of nature for you. It may be a solitary tree on a city street or a forest walk, a place where the sky seems bigger than usual or a bench by a lake. It is your place, and you may wish to return to it repeatedly.

2. Once there, pause and notice what you see and hear. Feel the earth under your feet. Touch what you can. Take in the miracle of the natural world and know that you are in it.

3. Speak your "yes." You are choosing to open to God. You are asking the earth and this particular spot in the natural world to bear witness to your "yes."

CHAPTER TWO

FACING OUR FEARS

For God hath not given us the spirit of fear,
but of power and of love, and of a sound mind.
—2 Timothy 1:7 (KJV)

Joan and I sat facing each other in the small room that is my office. She had just told me that she was thinking of divorcing her husband, but was afraid to go ahead with it. I listened as she talked about how they were always arguing, how little they had in common, and how much it would hurt the children. Suddenly she started crying. The hardest part, she confided through her tears, was that she couldn't pray anymore. Her faith was important to Joan, but she'd stopped attending Mass and she'd given up praying. She was afraid to open the divorce decision to God.

For over thirty years I have listened to people's stories in my office. Whether people seek me out for spiritual direction or psychotherapy, fear is often in the room with us. We may not name our silent companion, as Joan did, but behind the pain, underneath the anger, between the poles of wanting change and resisting change, sits fear. I've learned to sense its presence and to bring it out from its hiding place so we can look at it squarely and explore it.

Being afraid is a basic human experience. There are many forms of danger, and the fear response helps us protect ourselves and make ourselves less vulnerable. But fear has an unhealthy aspect as well. It tends to expand beyond its boundaries and to out-live its usefulness. The painful relationship of many years ago, for example, may prevent us from taking any chances on a new rela-tionship. Present fears often arise from such past places of pain.

As we consider our *willingness* to open to the Spirit and to make decisions informed by the Spirit, it's important to pay attention to the fears we have about being willing. What kinds of fears are stirred up by the thought of opening ourselves to God and to a wisdom beyond our own? Many of us have some fear about trusting God with our decisions, fear about allowing God to create with us the path we will take. We might hesitate to examine such fears too closely. I think looking at them will free us. We will be free to decide how important they are and how much influence they have in our lives.

Even a little fearfulness can keep us from moving ahead in our decision making. If we're apprehensive about something, we often avoid it. We hold on tight where we are. But until we examine our fears and our resistances, we give them too much power. Our unexamined fear sets limits on what we know about ourselves, on what we open to God. Evagrius Ponticus, a fourth-century desert father, wisely said, "If you want to know God, learn to know yourself first." When we avoid places in ourselves where fear dwells, we limit our knowing of ourselves and our freedom to become who we can be.

Fear limits our choices. When we're guided by fear, we can't hear the Spirit's whispers; consequently, we fail to perceive the steps we need to follow to take the best path. We might even avoid something as straightforward and simple as gathering information. Learning about anything from graduate schools to Alcoholics Anonymous (AA) meetings can be intimidating if we allow fear to take hold. It's easy to postpone doing a little research, blaming it on our busy lives, when the uncomfortable truth is that something inside us is afraid and is resisting making any move at all. But at the same time there's also a part of us that *wants* to move forward in spite of our fears, that is yearning for more wisdom in our decisions and more support on the path. There is a part of us that would love to trust a wisdom greater than our own. Pulled in two directions at once, we can wind up feeling thoroughly divided.

Let's begin by showing respect for those feelings of fear, those places of resistance. Let's look at them directly and ask: Who are you? What are you about? Where do you come from? Can we talk? They have important things to tell us if we listen. Significant life stories are contained within them. These stories still shape our lives, and, unless we pay attention to them, we won't know if the way they shape us is helpful or not. We won't know how much we're handicapped by them or how much truth they may still hold for us.

When Joan was considering divorce, she had closed herself off from God. She needed to ask where that resistance came from, what she was afraid of. As she looked at her life story, she realized that she had grown up believing she had to be "good" in order to be loved by God. Brought up by parents who seemed to show love to her only when she was very well-behaved, she had signed on to be "good" her whole life. Inside her resided a small child who was afraid she couldn't trust God to understand and love her if she went through with a divorce.

Someone once told me that he had a "room of resistance" inside himself where he didn't want to go. It was a room to which he alone held the key. Gradually, he said, he was learning how to open the door, and gently examine the fear and resistance that lived there. He was beginning to grow compassionate toward his own story. He felt tender toward the child he had been and to the younger man who struggled to make his way in the world. When we look at the "rooms of resistance" in our life stories, we too can grow more loving and compassionate to the stories within those rooms.

When William Penn, the Quaker founder of Pennsylvania, was designing governance for his new colony in the late seventeenth century, he wrote in one of his reflections, called *Fruits of Solitude,* "Let us then try what Love will do: For if Men did once see we Love them, we should soon find they would not harm us." Penn wanted the colony to be a "Holy Experiment" where a loving respect for each citizen would provide tolerance for people of many religions and races.

I suggest that we use "Let us try what Love will do" as the mantra for our own holy experiment. Choosing to be guided by love, rather than fear, helps us see our fears more clearly and compassionately and understand more about the power they've exerted in our lives. Being guided by love enlarges our vision for decision making.

St. John wrote, "There is no fear in love, but perfect love casts out fear" (1 John 4:18). Even when our love isn't perfect, it empowers us to see more clearly and step forward with courage. Choosing to approach our fears with love frees us to have greater trust in a God of love. When we struggle with our fears, we're struggling on behalf of that self within us that wants to open to love. That's our truest self, the person we've been created to be, and whom, deep within, we are longing to become.

In the following sections, I describe four areas of fear and resistance that turn up frequently in our decision making. You may identify others that are uniquely yours. All of them are about the struggle to grow more fully into whom we've been created to be, and all are about our relationship with God. Which areas are most familiar to you?

FEAR OF NOT BEING IN CHARGE

The human fear of not being in charge of our own decisions and our own lives may be the most common of our fears about involving God in our decisions. Even when we're confused, we sometimes resist asking for advice, even for advice from God, and we certainly don't want anyone else to make the decision for us. We would not be in control then, and who knows where we'd wind up? We're afraid that we might not like that place at all!

This is an understandable reaction. Becoming independent, self-directed adults with a sturdy sense of selfhood is a major focus of maturation. I believe that many of us are afraid of losing our sense of self-definition if we invite God's guidance into our lives. We're afraid we'll become less than we have been, diminished or dependent by leaning on the One who is more. After all, we may have spent years on the psychologically important tasks of separating from our parents and developing ego strength. Western culture respects independent, self-motivated people and looks pityingly on those who are self-effacing or dependent. The compound word *self-effacing* even suggests an "erased face"—not the direction in which we want to go.

We are needlessly afraid. To discern our path with God's guidance calls for our whole being. Enlisting the God of wisdom in our decision making inevitably draws us to become *more,* not less. It calls for using all the strength and giftedness we were created with. To discover the path that is best for us in our unique circumstances, we need to fully participate in the process.

Yes, there is something to be lost here, but it is not true selfhood. It is a false sense of self. This false sense of self says, "It's all up to *me. I* must get it right." It is afraid of stumbling or not getting it right, and so it tries still harder, insisting that it's in charge. When we let go of the attempt to manage it all ourselves, we don't find that God takes charge and we become passive recipients of God's plan. Instead, we become involved and active discerners together with God. As active discerners, being "in control" is a moot point. There is no control. We can only bring all we are to the effort of wise decision making.

My journey from carefully guarding my independent decision making to inviting God to enter into it was a long one. As a young adult, I thought that managing my life was hard, but I certainly didn't want to upset my careful balance of career, family, home, and community activities. I was afraid that God's "plan" for my life, if I really paid attention, would take me into a life that couldn't coexist with the one I had. I was afraid that God would insist on my doing something extraordinary, like going to Africa to serve those in need. It didn't occur to me that God works with what is real, that the reality of my two young children would be woven into my life with God. It didn't occur to me that God would help enrich the life I had so it would be easier to balance all the pieces and live a life truer to my real self.

In spite of my determination to be in charge of my life, I also wanted to let down my barriers. I wanted to be closer to the Spirit; I wanted something more. Very slowly, I began to notice everyday sacred moments and to seek out sacred places where I might feel that the Spirit was present. When my carefully balanced life got unbalanced, as carefully balanced lives do at times, it began to be natural to invite God to enlarge my understanding of the situation, to ask God to show me what my truest self could be.

I discovered that I had to be active in discernment. I needed to bring all I was and all the circumstances of my life into consideration of how to live. I found ways to live out God's love and compassion for others right where I was. Bolstered by a wisdom greater than my own, it was easier to make decisions that were right and true for my life.

FEAR OF CHANGE

When we begin a discernment process and brace ourselves to make decisions, we are entering a time of change. Some things will drop away, others will rise up, and life will take unforeseen turns. Even when we carefully and thoughtfully conclude *not* to change a situation, such as turning down a job offer that would uproot our children from their schools and their friends, the process of considering it changes us internally.

We can be thoroughly unhappy with a situation, and still be afraid to change it. A *familiar* unhappy situation often feels much safer than the unknown. A few years ago I met with a man who was miserable and bored in his job as the office support person for a roofing and siding company, but he had stuck with it for years. Friends would suggest he find new work, but he didn't even want to think about that. The prospect was too intimidating. He wrapped himself in the unhappy security of the familiar and grew more and more depressed. Only when he received a mediocre performance review, in which the word *dismissal* was used, did he finally wake up. He examined his feelings about his job, and realized how much he hated sitting in front of a computer all day. Eventually, he decided to apply for a job as a field estimator for his company, and, getting the job, he discovered that traveling around and meeting people suited him much better than office work. He wondered why he had waited so long to make a change.

Fear of change comes in many forms. Sometimes we're afraid that choosing to change will alter our sense of who we are. Letting go of a sense of identity can be scary. Who am I if I'm not defined by my child's needs, by my job, or by anger at my parents? Who am I if I'm not the wallflower, the class clown, the dedicated student? Who am I if I'm not the ever-helpful friend? If we put aside those "truths" we believe about ourselves, we don't know what we'll be left with.

The old self-understanding feels safer than the unknown. All change brings loss, and we might grieve the loss of old self-limiting stories even as we begin to recognize that they have limited us. It can be hard at first to appreciate the new freedom of growing into who we can become.

Sometimes our lives feel just right and we'd like to keep things just as they are. Even so, change will still come to us. We might well be afraid of its arrival. When the last child leaves home, when a spouse dies, when the business closes, unwanted change comes. Our decision then will be how to live with what has changed. We will need the divine Guide to learn to live amid the grief.

My friend Glenn recently married and is blissfully rebuilding an old country house for himself and his wife. He loves working on the house, nailing on the new siding and pausing to watch the sun set over the mountain. He confided recently that he's as happy as he has ever been. He is contented. Contentment, he says, is living in the peace of the present moment no matter what changes might come.

In the end, we have to allow change, even courageously welcome it, because we know it is the only way to satisfy our innate longing to grow. The resistance to change and the longing to grow into a better life are so balanced that sometimes it seems impossible that either side could give way. The tipping point comes when the Guide teaches us to trust just a bit more than we fear.

FEAR OF TRUSTING THE GUIDE

Have you ever participated in a "trust walk"? It's an experience of learning to trust as you are blindfolded and then led by a partner, upstairs, downstairs, outdoors, and around all kinds of barriers. It can be fun, but nervous laughter typically accompanies this exercise. For some participants, it is very difficult to depend so completely on another. Others walk confidently with their partner, trusting they'll be led safely through and around any obstacles until they reach their destination.

Trusting the Spirit's guidance is like the trust walk of a lifetime. We aren't blindfolded, and yet we often don't know where we're going or even understand where we are. Trusting that there is a wise Guide, with love and greater understanding than our own, may seem just about impossible.

One reason may lie in what we've been taught about God. As children, we may have learned that God is hard to please and quick to judge. Even when children are taught to say "God is love," if the religious atmosphere of childhood belies that statement, it won't stick. Trying to please a frowning, judgmental divinity may lead to obedience, but it doesn't lead to heart-deep trust. It is the difference between my second-grade teacher who ran a strict classroom of thirty lively children with frequent threats and absolutely no warmth, and my father's love of our family. Even when he reproved us children, he ended with a pat on the head. I always knew that his guidance was grounded in loving us.

Even if we weren't taught about a judgmental God, there are times when we can find ourselves to be disturbingly unlovable. We know we can be kind, generous, and compassionate, but we can also be mean-spirited, unforgiving, and self-centered. We conclude that sometimes we don't deserve love. A God who pours out love unconditionally is simply too hard to believe in.

I find it helps to think of ourselves as made up of layers, as an onion is. The outer layer—our public face—is how we appear to those around us. In the middle layer we hide our brokenness, grievances, the places of rage, and the sharp unkindnesses we are capable of. Fewer people see that, although the evidence sometimes pops out when we don't want it to. But deep inside us is the place God can see, even when we don't. That's the heart of who we are, our truest self, the one made to receive and give love. It's the layer where graces and gifts lie waiting to be discovered.

God's loving gaze takes in all our layers. With God's prompting, we, too, can see the innermost layer and accept that we are worthy of being loved unconditionally. The poet William Blake wrote, "And we are put on earth a little space, / That we might learn to bear the beams of love." Trusting God's beams of love, accepting those beams, is sometimes hard, but learning to trust the love helps us become the person we were created to be.

The second reason we may have trouble trusting God is in reaction to those times when we have prayed desperately for a desired outcome, and it didn't happen. What we wanted was unquestionably a good thing, yet God didn't bring it to pass. A friend who devoted her life to building peaceful communities got cancer and died at age forty. Prayers didn't change the course of her disease. Or a worthy project—an organic farm or a day center for the homeless—was a disappointing failure. We'd prayed for the project's success. Or maybe we didn't call it praying, but we truly longed for this *good* to be successful. But volunteers didn't sign up or the money didn't come in. Can God's faithful love for us really be trusted in the face of such heartbreak? I believe that it can.

What we have is a paradox: The evidence of God's creative love, presence, and activity in the world actually depends on our trusting in God and stepping out ourselves. It lies in our taking the risk when we don't know how it will turn out. Sometimes the evidence of God's presence is in the effort that we make. Our willingness to step forward empowers love, even in the face of failed projects and tragic deaths. What if God's trustworthiness is separate from having prayers answered and plans succeed? What if God is Light and Love, not a guarantee of certain outcomes?

In spiritual discernment, we open ourselves to receive as much as we can of the Light to show us the way. We are participants with God in creating the path we walk. Love's trustworthiness lies in its constancy, no matter what the shape of our lives. God's trustworthiness is in the ongoing availability of divine wisdom and love.

A FINAL FEAR: GOD, ARE YOU ANYWHERE?

In *The Silver Chair,* one of C. S. Lewis's fantasy books about the country of Narnia, there is a lovable character named Puddleglum. A lugubrious, drooping fellow, Puddleglum always expects the worst to happen. In *The Silver Chair,* he and the children who are the book's heroes are on a quest through the mysterious "Underland" when they are captured by the wicked queen. She knows they belong to the upper world, where the sun shines and Aslan the lion is the good lord of Narnia. Trying to tempt them into becoming her followers, not Aslan's, she throws a hypnotic incense onto the fire and chants, "There is no sun, there is no Aslan" over and over again.

The children succumb and slowly begin to repeat the words after her, but Puddleglum fights free of the enchantment. He walks over to the fire and stamps it out with his bare feet. Then he says:

> Suppose we have only dreamed, or made up, all those things—trees and grass and sun and moon and stars and Aslan himself. Suppose we have. Then all I can say is that the made-up things seem a good deal more important than the real ones. Suppose this black pit of a kingdom of yours is the only world. Well, it strikes me as a pretty poor one.... We're just babies making up a game, if you're right. But four babies playing a game can make a play-world which licks your real world hollow. That's why ... I'm on Aslan's side even if there isn't any Aslan to lead it. I'm going to live as like a Narnian as I can even if there isn't any Narnia.

Like Puddleglum and the children, we may sometimes be susceptible to a voice in our heads that repeats, "There is no God. There is no Light illuminating the world." The question "God, are you anywhere?" is often raised by those who would like to open to the wise Spirit that can see further than they can but who have doubts about the existence of such an entity. Some of us have a strong and unshakeable faith in the reality of God, but many of us struggle with what writer Madeleine L'Engle has called an "attack of atheism." Often this is a very private, interior struggle.

While we can rejoice if our faith in God is strong, we can, like Puddleglum, also choose to live as if God is real when we simply don't know. In other words, we can choose to open ourselves to the mysterious Other even when we question whether it's there at all. During an "attack of atheism," we can still choose to live by the love of Christ; by the light of Buddha, the Enlightened One; by the precepts of Yahweh. How we choose to live says more about the reality of God in our lives than does the certainty of the beliefs we hold.

Today we have turned the words *believe* and *belief* into words having to do with what we *think,* words of the head, but they were originally words of *feeling,* words of the heart. They are connected to the early northern European words for love and trust. Likewise, *creed,* a formal statement of belief, traces its ancestry back to the Latin *cor,* or heart. Perhaps we need to return to the heart and what it knows and yearns for when we consider the presence of the Holy One in our lives and in the universe. What does your heart know—even if your analytical head raises all kinds of questions? What is your heart drawn to? What does your heart believe?

Practices for Finding Your Way

These practices focus on looking at our fears with respect and learning from them. They will help you acknowledge them and perhaps diminish their power. Journaling is a valuable tool in these experiences.

THE NAMING GAME
We begin by facing and naming the resistances and fears that block our willingness to open to God and prevent us from receiving God's wisdom.

1. As you reflect on the four main sections of this chapter, do you recognize any of your own fears and resistances? If there are several, choose one to address.
2. Create a name or an image for the fear you are focusing on. For example, you may be dealing with

the "judge," or perhaps you decide to name your resistance something like Suspicious Sal. Perhaps you can create an image for your fear. (What does the judge look like anyway?) Maybe you imagine it as a boulder blocking your path or a large, bristling cactus that you don't want to touch.

3. Take a good look at it. What does it look like and what do you know about where it came from? Has it been helpful to you in the past? Is there any part of it that is useful to you in your present life?

4. Consider what would be different about your life if you relinquished this fear or diminished its power. What might change about your life? Imagine your fear shrinking in size (the incredible shrinking boulder!) until it is the size you want it to be for now.

5. When you complete this exercise, take a couple of deep breaths, and then slowly release them. If you've been sitting, stand up and stretch; move around or go outdoors. This can help you bring the experience to a close.

THE ROOM

This practice uses the imagination to move you beyond living in a room dominated by fear.

1. Imagine a house that has rooms for many experiences. There is a room for delight, a room for work, a room for playfulness. There are rooms for peacefulness and for anger, and one windowless room, down in the basement, for fear. Picture the house as completely as you wish, but without entering the rooms.

2. Without entering the fear room, state loudly and firmly, "I don't live there anymore." Repeat it several times. Perhaps you *visit* there occasionally, but let yourself feel what it is like to not live there anymore.

3. Picture yourself entering one of the other rooms of the house that you will find rewarding and satisfying. What do you find yourself doing there? How do you feel in that room?

4. After a little while, take a deep breath and release it slowly, bringing the practice to a close. You may want to stand and stretch, move around, or go outdoors.

Releasing Fear

Fear and resistance are held not just within the mind but within the whole body, so this practice engages the whole physical self in releasing them.

1. Sit comfortably, with your eyes closed or unfocused. Notice your breathing—not changing it, simply observing it. Notice the way you've chosen to sit. Does it stress or tighten any part of your body? Adjust your position to be comfortable.

2. Be aware of how you have been carrying tension within you. Perhaps it comes from a fear that we've named in this chapter. Perhaps it is another fear or resistance that keeps you from moving forward in your life. Acknowledge your desire to release it, not to carry it anymore.

3. Take a deep breath and release your breath slowly. You may wish to repeat words of release, a mantra such as "Let go, let go" or "I am releasing...." Taking another deep breath or so, let your body begin to relax. Perhaps your palms gently unfold and open, signaling your willingness to release fear and be open to the Spirit. Now allow relaxation to flow down your body, as you release tension in each part of your body. Notice what it feels like to release this tension.

4. Continue to repeat the mantra, noticing your quiet breathing and relaxed body. Remain quiet, allowing

the breathing and the mantra to settle your spirit. Stay with this practice longer than you think you need to.

Accepting Love

This meditative practice invites you to begin trusting a loving God. The only essential tool for the practice is your desire to relearn trust.

1. Sit quietly with the words below and let them sink into you. Stop reading and picture a loving God speaking with you gently and tenderly. Slowly reread these words several times.

   > Do not fear, for I have redeemed you; I have called you by name, you are mine. When you pass through the waters, I will be with you; and through the rivers, they shall not overwhelm you.... You are precious in my sight, and honored, and I love you. (Isaiah 43:1–2, 4)

2. Allow one word or phrase to repeat itself in you. Recognize your yearning for it to be true and for you to trust it. Stay with this practice longer than you think you need to.

Here we are, Loving One, Creator God,

half-awake to this astounding world,
half-awake to our own mysterious lives,
absorbing only drops of this richly layered life.

We want to notice more, to be alive
to who we are within,
to the stories and the dreams,
to the person we have been
and the one we can become.

To know what is real
we are ready to surrender
illusion, that painted comfort
which has been our friend.

We want to see what is true, what is real,
to hold as much as heart and mind can hold
of the world we live in
and whom we can become.

We want to be awake, God, to your opening of paths,
to create and participate
in this shaping of the way.

Here we are, Loving One, ready to begin.

PART II

ATTENTIVENESS

CHAPTER THREE

SURVEYING THE SITUATION

Hineini *(Here I am)*.
—*Exodus 3:4*

When my friends Phil and Mary Ann approached retirement, they gave considerable thought to what lay ahead. Mary Ann worked as a librarian and Phil taught in a technical college as an electrician, but what did they want in their future? This important question reminded Phil of what he had done with another big transition in his life. As a young man, he had given two years of voluntary service in Kenya before he started his career. He wondered if this retirement transition might be the time for another international experience. Phil and Mary Ann considered the idea carefully: They both had skills to offer and time to give. They had always lived simply and knew they could adapt to a variety of living conditions. They were ready for an adventure and mature enough to accept its challenges.

Eventually, they decided to apply to the Peace Corps and were assigned to Lesotho in southern Africa. A school there had asked for someone to create a library for them, and Mary Ann was just the person they needed. With books sent by friends back home, she built a substantial collection. The school also needed someone to set up a power-generating system based on wind and solar energy. Phil worked on that, helped maintain the school's buildings, and occasionally taught science and English. They both used more skills than they knew they had, and they returned to the United States after two years with a richly rewarding experience behind them.

When they reflect on those years, they recognize how much their successful experience depended on knowing themselves well and carefully evaluating their life circumstances as they made their decision. They needed to see their lives with clear eyes.

The art of knowing ourselves lies in facing what is real and true and seeing it clearly. Who we are, where we are now—that is the starting point for all our decisions. We need to know the truth about ourselves—but that is easier said than done. When I try to survey my self, I may be challenged by a lack of clearsightedness. Mirrors inform me of my appearance, but they don't tell my whole story or the truth about who I am.

There are many reasons for this lack of self-understanding. Sometimes we are simply too close to ourselves to see the truth about our lives clearly. Some truths are only visible at a distance. When astronauts circle the earth, for example, they can identify oceans and landmasses, polar icecaps and the lights from large cities; they don't see borders or national boundaries. They see no lines drawn between Canada and the United States, between China and Russia, between Israel and Lebanon. A powerful truth is visible to them—the interconnectedness of the whole earth—which is harder for us on earth to remember. That is why it is useful to take a long step back and, as the astronauts do, circle around our own planetary selves as we survey what is real. The practices at the end of this chapter are particularly helpful to us if we can be somewhat detached observers. While the truth we see may spark strong emotions, it is important not to color the truth to make ourselves more comfortable. Feelings carry their own truth, and we will focus on them in the next chapter.

I am using the word *survey* here deliberately. When a professional surveyor inspects a property, he is not judging whether the lot is beautiful. He is simply interested in accurately measuring its shape and edges. His truth is the accuracy of the plot's dimensions, and he wants to see that truth. When we survey ourselves, we, too, need accurate truths in our survey. We need to look at ourselves, our stories, our personalities, and our habits, and say, "Yes, there I am."

Our survey is further complicated because we are such enormously complex beings. What seems true one day is contradicted on the next. Sometimes I am a generous, warmhearted person, and sometimes, when I'm tired and overextended, I'm a definite negative on the compassion scale. It's hard to sort out which is the real me. I wholeheartedly agree with my friend Andrew Woff who wrote, as he pondered his own complexities and contradictions,

> Being me is a complicated business, God.
> So many needs, desires, hopes and fears;
> So much history that has shaped me....
> So much faith; so much doubt.
> So much of me that comes to the Light,
> So much of me that hides in deep shadow....

One way to approach our own complex selves is through the history that has shaped us: our own stories. We all have stories. These are the givens—our personal history, the facts and situations that we know to be true. Even if they are sometimes contradictory and mysterious, we can say, "Yes, this is my story." As we pay attention to them and invite the Light to illuminate them, we find we know more than we thought we did. We see patterns and themes emerging that can help us know ourselves. We may even recognize how a divine Being beyond ourselves is active in our lives.

SURVEYING PAST AND PRESENT FOR FUTURE'S SAKE

What has already happened, the past, is an unchangeable part of our story. It is a reality. However, it is what we learn from the past and what we do with it that creates opportunity for change and movement. From the past we shape the present and create the future. Past, present, and future are useful divisions, but our daily lives are not so easily divided into those three neat segments. They flow into each other. The past is alive in the present and may pop up in the future and need reinterpretation. Like Charles Dickens's Scrooge encountering the Ghosts of Christmas Past, Present, and the silent Future, we, too, live with our past, our present, and our unknown future all at the same time.

To begin the hard work of knowing ourselves, a thoughtful survey is the first step. The question "Who am I?" is naturally overwhelming, and most answers we come up with seem incomplete and contradictory. However, if we look at what we do know, rather than focusing on all that is a mystery about ourselves, we can begin. After all, some things about ourselves, such as our personalities, our innate gifts, and other skills we have learned through practice are relatively stable over time. Let's begin with them.

My daughter Alisa's first job after college was to develop a program to bring young people from various ethnic and socioeconomic groups together to learn from each other. It was a fairly solitary job—she was given an office by herself and a phone, and told to go to it. While she had success with the program, the most useful thing she gained was self-knowledge. My daughter is an extrovert who likes being with people and draws energy from those interactions. Through the frustrations of working alone, she discovered just how important collaborative effort was to her creativity and her job satisfaction. This helped her make a decision about her future. Her next job was as an environmental educator—a park ranger in Yellowstone National Park. She answered questions, gave talks, and guided walks for visitors all day long. She was part of a team and interacting with people constantly. She loved it.

Once I met with a young woman whose parents had urged her to see a counselor because they thought she was stuck in a rut working as an administrative assistant at a local college. Although she had friends, she didn't go out much. She wondered aloud if she was missing something, or if something was wrong with her. But then she told me that the best part of her life was taking free classes at the college. Her face lit up when she told about the music appreciation class last term, the class on introduction to personality theory she was taking now, and that next year she'd set her sights on Shakespeare. We talked about how much she had enjoyed doing projects in high school, and she remembered reading the encyclopedia for fun when she was a young child. We acknowledged that intellectual curiosity was an important part of who she was; she wasn't "stuck in a rut" but enjoying the fun of learning. For now, she decided, she was exactly where she wanted to be.

In addition to reflecting on our experiences, we can find other ways to further our self-understanding. Personality inventories, such as the Myers-Briggs Personality Inventory or the Enneagram for Personality can help. While we are much more than a Myers-Briggs psychological type or an Enneagram number, we can use them to learn some fundamental things about ourselves. Both of these personality inventories help us gain understanding of who we are as well as insight into our relationships and the kinds of activities and work we are best suited for. The Enneagram, in particular, teaches us about growing into more spiritual and emotional maturity.

Sometimes the hardest part of looking at ourselves is acknowledging our gifts. Skills we have learned over time are a little easier to accept—yes, I am a good tennis player, a skillful computer programmer, a careful driver, or an accomplished cook. We've worked on our gifts and have earned our skillfulness. But the essential giftedness of our being, which is innate, can be challenging to acknowledge as part of who we are. For example, Leah is seen by others as a wise and insightful woman who speaks clearly in difficult situations. She tends to see herself in negative terms, as the unwelcome voice who raises thorny issues that no one wants to face. In time, however, she may grow into the mature understanding that her clear insights are a developed gift.

Like a stiff new pair of shoes, which gradually become an easy fit, awareness of our own gifts needs time to become comfortable. What gift do you need to acknowledge? It could be a gift of leadership or administration, or a gift for listening or for music. Possibly you are gifted in spatial creativity (do you build?) or in verbal creativity (do you write?).

Surveying what is real and true also includes looking at present life circumstances. It involves our living arrangements, our responsibilities, our financial circumstances, our relationship to the community around us, and the presence or absence of friends and family. These facets of our lives may seem so obvious that we may wonder why they warrant special attention. But only by looking at them directly can we see how they shape our lives. Only by stepping back from the immediate present and seeing them with a degree of detachment can we discern what needs to change and what is best left as is. We may surprise ourselves and discover how to create something different for the future.

Remember that these circumstances of our present lives are true now, in this season of our lives. Yet they may change as we move into another season. For example, a woman who works part-time and is the mother of two middle school students reflected with me on the present realities of her life. She recognizes that to become a nurse—a profession she wants to pursue— she'll have to train for that work now, before the family has two college students to support. This is the time for her to make that shift. Through preparation, she can be working at a satisfying job six years from now, and her income will help the family's stretched finances when college starts.

When the present season of our lives is a hard one, it is especially helpful to recognize that seasons do change. The joy of having preschool children and seeing them develop and grow does not diminish the challenge of caring for them. A person near retirement may keep an unsatisfying job for the health benefits. Just two more years to Medicare! Clearly naming the seasons of our lives and acknowledging how long they'll last helps us decide what to do about them.

HOOKS AND ATTACHMENTS

In addition to looking at our past, present, and future, a survey of self includes looking at our hooks and attachments. We all have them, and they interfere with our clear understanding of past and present, and our clear vision for the future as well. We are *hooked* by situations that remind us of painful experiences from the past. We are *attached* to people, events, or things when we clutch them so desperately that we can't enjoy them or let go of them. Moreover, the places where we get hooked and the attachments we cling to can seriously cloud our judgment and discernment. They make it hard to see what is possible in our lives. But they are real and a key source of truth. We need to be able to see them to recognize the influence they have in our decision making.

Hooks often catch us unexpectedly. Themes from long ago that don't fit our present lives still tend to trip us up. We react to a present situation with a response based on something that happened in the past. It may have served us well then; it doesn't now. Hooks are the vulnerable Achilles' heel of our interactions with other folks. Like the Greek mythological hero Achilles, who could be killed only by an arrow through his heel, we, too, have places where we are especially vulnerable to being hurt. If we don't know what they are, they can shape our decisions uncon-sciously. When I was a child, I was often left out of schoolyard play. I was too quiet and bookish, and, besides, one year my mother was our classroom teacher! As a young adult, I some-times avoided the possibility of being passed over by withdraw-ing before that could happen. I eventually learned to recognize when I'd been hooked by old messages and to carefully release the wires that trapped me in old, unproductive patterns. And I am glad to report that the hooks are considerably less likely to catch me now than they were years ago.

Attachments also affect our ability to make decisions and to discern the right path. Only by naming those things we hold so tightly can we make wise choices about them: what to hang on to, what to grasp more lightly, and what to release. Only by examin-ing them can we discriminate between healthy closeness and a clutched-fist attachment. A healthy closeness between people allows spaces in their togetherness, spaces for each to grow. If I grasp another person too closely, I lose the ability to see him clearly; all my attention has gone into hanging on for dear life. We may clutch things as much as people—I am deeply attached to my garden, for example, and I wonder if I will ever be able to release it with grace.

A friend has given me a helpful metaphor for thinking about attachment and detachment. She developed tendonitis in her wrist and had to wear a brace, but she is an active woman and fretted at her limitation. Then she was told by her doctor to hold things more lightly and easily. My friend was surprised at what a difference it made for her, not only in her wrist pain, but in her whole attitude. Following her example, I decided to try holding things lightly as well. I didn't need to drop them, just relax my grip. And as I held my sandwich, my cat, my computer, my car keys more lightly, I began to see them more clearly, with a renewed appreciation for their unique place or service in my life. Is there something in your life that you need to hold more lightly? Is there a relationship, a possession, or an activity that you need to hold more lightly, even if you continue to value it?

WITH DIVINE LIGHT

Twelve Step programs harness the power of the self-survey as a way for us to change our lives. The Twelve Step process includes acknowledging our helplessness in dealing with addiction, confessing the need for a Higher Power, and facing the pain we have inflicted on others through our life choices. The Twelve Steps can lead to new life, but only to the extent that we see what is true and acknowledge the need for a Higher Power. All of us need the light and wisdom of a Higher Power so that we can see our lives clearly and choose with wisdom.

While I've emphasized the importance of stepping back from ourselves and observing as clearly as we can what there is to see, we also need to be tenderly understanding of ourselves. We need to look with tenderness at the stories, the vulnerabilities, the gifts, and the seasons of our lives. This tenderness is an echo of God's tender looking and loving acceptance. "The way to God," says Benedictine author Anselm Gruen in *Heaven Begins Within You,* "lies through the encounter with myself, through the descent into my reality." That is true, but so is the reverse—the way to our true selves lies in an encounter with a loving God. The way to our truest understanding of ourselves lies in our opening to God's love and acceptance of us.

The ancient prayer of *examen* is the spiritual legacy of St. Ignatius of Loyola, founder of the Society of Jesus. It provides a daily time for reflection, which helps us recall God's presence in all parts of our lives. This practice opens to a loving God all the events and feelings, hopes and disappointments, failures and successes of the day and tries to look at them with God's loving eyes. Such a practice can guide us here. We gently hold our lives before a loving Presence as we explore our stories, our hooks and attachments, our gifts and skills, and all facets of our life circumstances.

In the light of God's love, we can be both tender and clear-sighted in seeing ourselves. We can open ourselves to learning more about our truth and we can receive the strength, understanding, and vision we need to find our way. Like my friend with tendonitis, we can hold the truth both lightly and lovingly.

Practices for Finding Your Way

These practices offer a variety of ways to survey ourselves and our life situations. Begin with those that address your situation but consider all of them. Perhaps you don't know what changes you need in your life but just feel dissatisfied with the way it is now. Try a variety of practices. The truth you need might be hidden anywhere in your life.

Paying attention as a spiritual practice cannot be rushed, so do the following exercises slowly and allow time for them to sink in. The gifts from these exercises show themselves in the spaces you allow for pausing and reflecting. The spaciousness of pondering allows the Spirit to light up what is there. You may notice something you had never noticed before, or be surprised by an insight about something you thought you knew well. Wait. Let the Light come.

THE CIRCLE STORY

This first practice invites you to remember parts of your life story and consider what they offer you in your present discernment process. Look at yourself and your story with tenderness and loving-kindness. You are not judging, simply noticing that these things are true. Look on your story in the same way a God of infinite love looks on you.

1. Take a large sheet of paper and draw a large circle. (You might draw an open circle to show that the story

you are in is not completed.) Divide it into quadrants or thirds, or whatever best fits your age. Or you could divide the circle into sections representing the areas of your life (work, home, family, friends, and the like).

2. For each section of your life, recall one occasion or situation when the best self you are, your truest self, was strong and active, with a clear sense of the "rightness" of what you were doing, the way you were being or relating to others. You may have felt extraordinarily alive and fulfilled. You may have felt that the Spirit or Christ or the Light was present with you in some way. Briefly describe that experience in that section of your circle.

3. Then recall one experience of being blocked or tripped up by your own vulnerabilities for each section of your circle and write about it. For example, you may have caused pain to yourself or another. You may remember that experience with grief or regret but also look at it with gentle understanding.

4. After you've finished, reflect on the following questions:

> What threads run through these experiences of your best, truest self? What do they have in common? How do you feel as you recall them? What did you find satisfying and rewarding about these experiences?
> Do the vulnerable places that tripped you up in the past still hold you in their clutches today? How could you address them today? How do you feel as you recall them? What do they have to teach you now?

5. Set the paper aside for an hour or a day and then return to it. As you reflect on it again, recall your

desire to see your circle through God's eyes and offer that desire as your prayer. Do you have any new understandings about yourself?

THE ENERGY FIELD

Our energy rises and falls in accordance with multiple factors—mental, physical, emotional, or a combination of them. This exercise helps you to see how you are drained and filled with energy throughout your life.

1. Choose a significant area of your present life to examine. If there is an area in which you are discerning your way, begin there. (You might choose work, home, parenting, friendships or social life, fun and play, or your relationship with your spouse.)

2. Draw two columns on a sheet of paper. Label one DRAINS and the other FILLS. Consider with as much detail as you can all aspects of the area you are focusing on and write down whether they energize or drain you. The FILLS column includes whatever energizes and satisfies you, whatever is rewarding and refreshing to you. The DRAINS column contains whatever empties you out or frustrates you. For example, if work is your focus, you might list *coworker* in the DRAINS column, and *hours with customers* in the FILLS column. Or perhaps it would be reversed. Don't forget to include the environment, people, hours, and the type of activity in this area. You might also find that something belongs in both columns. For example, as an introvert, I find public presentations to be draining, but speaking and leading a group on a subject I am passionate about is tremendously energizing.

3. Create a scale of 1 to 5, indicating the comparable level of filling and draining that is going on for each

of the factors you are considering. For me, public presentations would be a five on FILLS but only a three on DRAINS.

4. Continue with this process until you have named everything involved in this one area of your life. Take a break and then repeat it with other areas of your life, as many as seem right for you.

5. Put the scale aside for an hour or a day. When you pick it up again, pause to open yourself prayerfully to receive whatever understanding or wisdom may be revealed. Consider what patterns emerge. What are the most important factors that either drain or fill you with energy? Do they turn up in multiple areas? What are you learning about yourself?

A LITANY OF GIFTS AND SKILLS

Although we usually understand gifts to be inborn and skills to be developed through practice, they do overlap, and I place them together here in one exercise. This is a very simple practice that can be done over several weeks.

1. List as many of your gifts and skills as you can. Do not make comparisons or judgments. If you think you play the piano badly, still list it! Include qualities of who you are, not just what you do, such as *a gift for listening* or *empathy* or *the gift of laughter*.

2. Then add gifts and skills that you are not using now. Include both those you used in the past and those you have never used but believe you have somewhere deep inside you. (Perhaps you used to paint but haven't done it in years. Perhaps you've always believed you could be a builder, but you never explored that path.)

3. Ask friends or family members what skills or gifts they see within you. Explain that you are doing a

personal survey—and tell them you want the truth about what they see in you. They may want time to think about your question so they can answer it well.

4. Revisit your list over a period of weeks, adding to it as fully as you can. It may take some time to accept yourself as such a treasure house. You do not need to use all these gifts, but it is important to acknowledge their existence. Open your treasure list of gifts and skills to God in any way that seems right for you, acknowledging, "This is within me." How might these gifts and skills shape your decision making?

THIS SEASON OF LIFE

While each stage or season of our lives brings changes, sometimes we don't recognize the freedoms and limitations different seasons offer. In this exercise you will look at the present and discover how it has both limited and freed you.

1. Specify the season of life you are in right now. While there are broad life stages that are widely recognized (early adulthood, parenting preschoolers, retirement, etc.), you might need to be creative in describing the unique season you are in now. It could be the "newcomer in town" or the "leader who is no longer leading" phase of your life.

2. Reflect on the limitations that are built into this stage of your life. These may be in areas of responsibility, relationship (family or others), economic security, health, or energy levels.

3. Reflect on the freedoms you have in this stage of your life. Sometimes freedoms are more challenging to identify than limitations, particularly if the new freedom involves diminishment (such as the loss of a

spouse). You still have the freedom to choose how you live with the loss.

4. Sometimes the same reality both limits and opens your life. Retirement or job loss can severely limit your spending, but open you to a different way of living (less shopping at the mall and more use of library books, videos, and computer services; less eating out and more experimentation in the kitchen). What aspects of this season both limit and free you?

5. As you reflect on what you have written, use it to remember your desire to live this season guided by God's wisdom and light. What would it be like to live the limitations gracefully? What would your life look like if you really embraced the freedoms offered by this season?

LISTENING TO THE INNER SELF

We will come to God only on a path that goes through sincere self-encounter, through listening to our thoughts and feelings, to our dreams, to our body, our concrete lives, and our relationships with other people.

—*Anselm Gruen,* Heaven Begins Within You

When Solomon became the king of Israel, he offered a sacrifice at the high holy place of Gibeon. There he was given a dream, and in his dream Yahweh appeared to him and asked him to name his desire—what he most wished to receive. Solomon replied, "Give your servant a discerning heart to govern your people and to distinguish between right and wrong" (1 Kings 3:9, NIV).

Like Solomon, we need a discerning heart. Discerning with our hearts means paying attention to our feelings and our longings. It focuses on the truth we *feel*. It focuses on our emotions. But that understanding of heart-deep truth isn't profound enough to encompass all that Solomon was asking for. Other biblical translations of this story recount his request for "an understanding *mind*," and describe God's gift to him as "a wise and discerning *mind*" (3:12, NRSV).

Today we often separate the knowing of the heart and the knowing of the mind, and we might wonder which one Solomon was asking for. I think he was asking for a kind of understanding that goes beyond the heart's felt truth and the mind's rational truth. A wise old man once told me he imagined "the wings of the mind coming down and settling into the heart." Such truth seems to come from a place right at the center of who we are, deeper than thought and feeling. It is intuitive knowing. Often described as an insight that we can't fully explain or justify, intuitive understanding leaps over our reasoning, and even over our feelings, and lands in a place of simply *knowing what we know.* Trying to describe it to others, we might call it a flash of understanding or an "aha" moment. Creative work, for example, from scientific understanding to artistic pursuits, depends on paying attention to these intuitive leaps of understanding. Though we can try to confirm our intuitive knowing by further observation, it is important to simply be attentive to this source of knowing.

The past chapter invited us to step back from ourselves and our lives to become careful observers, using the light and wisdom of God to understand what we observed. It used the image of astronauts circling the planet Earth. In this chapter we come down from that circling spaceship and explore the interior world. We'll look at our feelings, thoughts, visions, and the messages of our bodies. Like miners with headlamps, we'll tap into inner knowing, searching for the inner truths we may not know that we know. The word *intuition* comes from the Latin word *intueri,* which means to look within or contemplate. We'll look within for our own inner truths in many ways throughout this book, and a new understanding might come at any time. But let's begin here with a few questions.

Consider an area of your life needing a decision. Ask yourself, "What do I know deep inside me that relates to this decision, even if I can't explain it? What do I already know about myself and about the situation I am in that I need to pay attention to here?" As you continue reading, you might return to these questions and your responses again and again, noticing how your understanding is growing.

Listening to Heart and Mind

Although honoring intuitive knowing is important, we also need to look at thinking and feeling as individual, separate sources of truth. Considering how we think or how we feel about something is a familiar process. How often do you say, "I think ..." or "I feel ..." in the course of a single day? And don't you generally tend to favor one of them over the other? Our individual personalities tilt us toward leaning on our emotions or on our reasoning in decision making, though we know we need to consult with both heart and head.

When couples have to make a decision together, these personality differences come to the fore. For example, Don carefully thinks through the pros and cons of all his decisions while his wife, Dawn, responds from her heart. When they think about buying a house, Don focuses on its practical aspects—the distance he will have to commute to work, the amount of lawn maintenance he'll have to do, and the cost of replacing the siding. Dawn, however, falls in love—with the kitchen, the view, and the backyard. Because this decision is a big one, both Don and Dawn also have to put their natural preferences aside and approach this decision in a way that comes to them less easily. Don has to consult his heart, asking himself how he *feels* about this house—how he likes the backyard and the view. Dawn must step back and evaluate the kitchen's storage space and carefully examine the room layout and size. Only then can they conclude that this house, at this time, is right for them.

Our culture is pragmatic, so we tend to respect reasoned conclusions more than conclusions based on emotions. A couple could decide to buy a house without even acknowledging that they each have strong feelings about it. They could conclude that it fits their needs and price range, and sign an agreement immediately. In making decisions, however, we need to give our feelings as much attention as our thinking and let them play an equal role. Both functions are part of good discernment practice.

It's wonderful when our hearts and our heads are so much in agreement that we might not even notice that a decision has been made. But when there's a conflict between heart and mind, it can be very painful. Then we need to give the conflict all our attention, examining our feelings and thoughts with care.

For example, Esther is deeply in love. She wants to spend her life with the man she loves, and he with her. But she has always pictured herself having children, and he is very sure he does not want any. Their hopes for their lives are very different. At first when they talked about a life together, Esther tried to ignore the questions her mind kept raising about children, but finally she acknowledged what her mind already knew—that this lovely man is not someone with whom she can build her life. While they love each other, their plans for living simply do not mesh.

Often the hardest part of a decision is the *timing* of a particular step. When it is a big step, like having a baby, changing jobs, or moving into a retirement home, it will be much harder to adjust to it if it is not yet the right time. Sometimes, as in the move to a retirement home, the mind knows the direction in which we're moving, but the heart isn't quite ready for it. Perhaps, as in starting a family, the heart is eager, but the thoughtful mind says it is not the right time.

I have friends who are suffering because their dearly loved adult son has a drug problem. They've supported and encouraged his efforts to fight the addiction, allowing him to move in with them, and they've paid for his treatment again and again. But at the same time they both know they are fast approaching a painful, even anguished decision to say to their son, "No more," forcing him to be responsible for himself, even if the consequences are painful for all of them. Together, the couple has concluded that a boundary needs to be established, although their hearts have not caught up with their heads. But sooner or later, although they continue to love him, they will reach the point of telling him he must leave home. The time must be right for that step.

In decision making, attending fully to our thoughts and feelings can't be done hastily. We need to give much time and care to the process. If you are pondering a specific decision as you read this, pause now and ask yourself, "How do I *feel* when I consider this possible choice? Or what about this other possibility? What does my heart know?" Listen to yourself; write down your feelings and the emotions that come to the surface. Likewise, consider all the reasons why you *think* possibility A or B should be the one to pursue. List these reasons. Rank them on a scale of 1 to 10. What are you learning about yourself?

LISTENING TO DREAMS AND VISIONS

Dreams come to us when we're awake or asleep, and both kinds come bearing gifts. To be attentive to our inner truths, therefore, we need to pay attention to both the dreams of our sleep and those of our waking hours.

Sometimes the dreams of our waking hours are dismissed as just daydreams, as something with no substance that we can safely ignore. But these daytime dreams always hold some truth worth noticing. What truths are held in your daydreams?

Dreams and visions have always been places that open into deeper understanding and enlightenment. They have been experiences of being called by God, as when Moses heard a voice coming from the burning bush, or when St. Francis of Assisi heard Jesus's voice commanding him, "Rebuild my church, which is broken." Taking those words literally, Francis went out and repaired an old stone chapel, and then founded the Franciscans, an order of mendicant friars whose witness to poverty helped to rebuild the medieval church of the thirteenth century.

These are awe-inspiring visions, but what about individual dreams for our ordinary lives? My friends Mary Lou and Rod dreamed of creating a small retreat house on their old farm. They imagined renovating an unused shed and adding a sleeping loft and a tiny kitchen. They pictured a wood stove and a large picture window where guests could look across the fields. Music and books would be available on the shelf beneath the window. Today, many years later, the cottage is warm and welcoming, a quiet oasis often booked weeks in advance. Offering this retreat space has given them all the joy they thought it would when they were dreaming about it. For Mary Lou, following the dream was an important step in her life journey. Eventually, she resigned from her teaching job and began study to become a spiritual director and retreat leader. Through this journey she has become more completely whom she is called to be in this season of her life.

If I ask, "What do you dream of? What path do you imagine opening before you?" do you have an answer? Do you allow yourself to dream while you're awake? Imagining what could be or having a dream for an alternative way of life is a powerful tool for discernment. Noticing what we dream about is noticing what we yearn for, even if we think it's completely out of reach. Dreams, even our vaguest hopeful glimpses, carry something of the true authentic self God created us to be. They can call us as surely as the burning bush called Moses.

Sometimes dreams for our lives reflect the experiences we've had that hurt us or broke us in some way. A need for affection twists into possessiveness; the hungry ego always needs more approval. But if we go deep enough into the dream for our lives, we will find a unique child of God striving to be whole in the only way it knows. We will find a child of God who wants to use the unique giftedness that is its alone. If we lift our dreams and imaginings into the divine Light, its clarity will help us find the piece of the dream that reflects our authentic self.

To use this rich source of truth about ourselves, we need to free it. We often tether our dreams with all the good reasons why they're impossible to fulfill. We need to expand our perception of the possible and imagine freely. Grow accustomed to your dreams so they lose some of their aura of impossibility. Then, with the Spirit's guidance, you can discern how to move something of the dream's essence into your life.

Put down this book for a few minutes and consider various dreams you've had for your life. You may want to journal about them. Consider dreams you had when you were younger, and those that are alive in you now. What truth about you emerges in those dreams? What in the dreams can help you find your way forward now?

Dreams from our sleep are equally powerful sources of truth. Dreams while we are asleep are a gift from ourselves to ourselves. They carry something for our discernment, some insight or knowing that may not seem to make much sense to our conscious mind. We may need to live with the story within the dream for a while to perceive its wisdom.

Sometimes there is something we know that is buried deeper than our conscious minds or feelings can reach. We can't access it when we're awake, but then it appears in a nighttime dream. Dreams may also refer to an area of our lives that we have closed off. For many years, I dreamed repeatedly of a hand writing words on a paper as I read them. I didn't know it was my own hand I was seeing, but when I finally acknowledged my desire to be a writer and began writing, the dream stopped. I had brought my dream out of the nighttime shadows and into the light of day.

Unlike the daydreams of our waking hours, we can't decide to have a nighttime dream, nor can we necessarily remember it. However, we can invite a dream, or request one as we settle into sleep. We can keep a dream journal by the bed. Writing out the dream upon awakening helps us remember it so we can reflect on its meaning.

LISTENING TO THE BODY

Often our bodies know truths about our lives long before we are ready to acknowledge them consciously. In *Maps to Ecstasy: A Healing Journey for the Untamed Spirit,* writer and artist Gabrielle Roth calls us "absentee landlords of our own estate." "So many of us," she says, "are not in our bodies, really at home and vibrantly present there.... We live outside ourselves—in our heads, our memories, our longings." Although we may know a lot about how they function, I'm not sure how much attention we pay to our bodies. If I'm leaning into the past or the future, I'm missing both the present moment and my present embodied self. I'm absent to my own precious "estate."

Put down this book and try listening right now. What are the different parts of your body telling you? Where is there tension or tightness? Where is there pain, even a little? If your body could choose its position right now, what would it choose? For many years I've guided people in relaxation exercises, and I've discovered that people often don't know how to read their bodies' signals. They don't know they are tense until they relax.

We do notice when our bodies are extraordinarily energized or well-rested or when we are in pain or are sick. But usually we're not at those extremes. For the most part, we are somewhere in between. Let's say that I am at a party and my body complains that it is tired. Just being there is bringing on a headache, to say nothing of aching smile muscles. Yet I expect to keep on going despite these signs of fatigue. I don't want to hear my body telling me that I'm not really having a good time, that I wish I were at home, immersed in a good book. If I listened to my body, I might have to do something about its truth telling.

Learning how to read our bodies is crucial in making decisions. What signs does your body use to tell you it's at peace? What are the indications when it is troubled? A knot in the stomach or a tension headache are realities to be attended to. Our bodies are not new acquaintances; we have no excuse for not knowing how they communicate. If I begin to have a knot in my stomach as I'm trying to decide whether to go to the next party, I need to ask myself what it is about partygoing that is bringing on my distress. Perhaps the friends I am close to won't be there, or maybe that particular group gossips and complains, or maybe there's too much drinking. First we pay attention to the body's warning; then we explore what it means within the context of the decision we are making.

My friend Sandy has chronic fatigue syndrome. She finds it even harder to bear because her enthusiasm for working on projects is still boundless, but she can't do nearly as much as she used to. Her body complains loudly if she ignores it. She needs to pay attention both to her enthusiastic spirit and to her body's exhaustion as she makes decisions about a new way of living for this season of her life. Discovering a way of being involved in the work she loves while still protecting her health is one of the hardest challenges she's ever faced.

Listening to our bodies doesn't only bring us news of limitations. When we have a passionate longing or a dream we could turn into reality, we experience it physically. We're energized by the idea, the possibility of making it happen. Springing to our feet, we charge ahead. Sometimes there is a real physical ache as we yearn for what we want to do or be. Our bodies—and especially our hands—express the yearning through opening, reaching, spreading gestures. What longing, what dream do you feel your body reaching for? How does your body express it?

A Depth of Passion

When we're attentive to our inner selves, we might discover something that stirs a real passion, such as a cause or a purpose. It may be a creative art, an injustice to protest, a contemplative way of life, or the care of a child. It draws us irresistibly. Swept along by such a forceful passion, our decisions are life-giving. Such passion has the energy of the river near my home after a heavy rainstorm: Branches, leaves, and all kinds of flotsam are swept along by the power of the water.

My ninety-seven-year-old friend Ted was captured and spent World War II in China in a prisoner-of-war camp because he was thought to be a U. S. intelligence agent. The suffering and brutality of the POW camp changed his life. It released a passion in him: The prison and the war, he discovered, were the epitome of everything he wanted to stand against. When he was freed after the war and returned to the United States, he spent the rest of his life promoting peace and working against violence. As a professor at Colgate University, he founded a Peace Studies program there. He marched, wrote books and thousands of letters, traveled, demonstrated, and spoke out publicly for his cause. Once he attended a Ku Klux Klan rally so he could talk with both the Klansmen and the angry protesters. And, as an old man, he traveled repeatedly through the troubled Balkans, eventually helping to found the Balkan Peace Studies Center.

Ted's passion played out in many settings but it all sprang from the same root—a longing to promote peace and nonviolence. It was grounded so deeply in him that it became the very purpose for which he lived. It swept through his life with the force of a river, energizing and empowering him.

Like my friend Ted, when we listen deeply and persist in our listening, we can unveil a passion, something that we care about intensely, something we can live for. We find that we can say, "This, *this*, I will stand for." The bumper sticker I saw a few days ago had a picture of the earth next to the slogan *Love your mother*. Now there's a big enough passion! There are many ways to live it out, too. What passion is big enough for your life?

In *Wishful Thinking: A Theological ABC*, Frederick Buechner wrote, "The place God calls you to is where your deep gladness and the world's deep hunger meet." The place we are deeply drawn to nourishes us with gladness and joy, and part of the joy is in giving ourselves to something beyond ourselves. Not just anything will do, but something that is rightly ours will satisfy and fulfill us. Performing community service, volunteering for a cause dear to our heart, or devoting ourselves to parenthood—when this is our own passion, we will experience a deep gladness.

Oftentimes, the shape of our lives keeps us from fully living out what we'd love to give ourselves to. If I have family responsibilities (small children and a spouse) or financial obligations (college debt), I might not be able to follow my desire to live in an ashram or a monastery. But I can go on silent retreats and practice meditation. I might not be able to become a full-time performance musician, but I can go on practicing and taking lessons and find my own unique way of playing music for others. There are many ways to live out a passion. And, as we pay attention to the wisdom we carry within us—the wisdom of heart, mind, and body; the wisdom of our dreams and our passions—we will discern the unique way of living that is ours for this season of our lives.

Practices for Finding Your Way

These are practices of noticing, of paying attention, and they need time for reflection. You may reflect on them, leave them for a time, and then return to ponder the questions again. Even when you're busy with something else, you will keep uncovering your truth.

WHAT THE BODY KNOWS

This practice invites you to become more aware of your body and to form a habit of paying attention to the wisdom within your body.

1. Sit comfortably and focus on your breathing. Observe your position and the parts of your body that seem most relaxed and those that seem most tense or tight. You are noting your body's status quo.

2. Recall a time in your life that was particularly hard, painful, or deeply confusing. Don't reenter that time, but notice what the remembering is doing within your body. Mentally scan down your body and notice where there is tension and tightness or pain. Has the memory changed your breathing? Notice the way you are holding your body. Stay with your body's response to this memory for a few minutes, then take a deep breath and let it go.

3. Recall a time in your life when things were particularly "right"; they were peaceful, happy, or very fulfilling. Let yourself reenter that time, if you wish, but notice any changes within your body. You may find yourself smiling, or perhaps there is a movement or gesture to express this experience. What is it?

4. Check in with your body several times a day for a week or longer. Stop what you are doing and notice your breathing, your body position, and the parts of your body that seem most relaxed and those that feel most stressed. What does your body know about what is going on in your life at that moment?

Two Ideal Days

Often we let our imaginations roam freely from one vaguely blissful state to the next. This practice puts our wandering imaginations at the service of concrete detail.

1. Imagine two ideal consecutive days of your life. By *ideal*, I mean very wonderful but based in realistic possibility. (You have not unexpectedly discovered that you are the heir to an enormous estate!) These days feel right for you and bring you much fulfillment. One could be a day at work and the other a day at home or on vacation.

2. Write out as much detail as you can about each portion of each day. For example, what is your ideal food? What clothes are you wearing? How are others relating to you? What work, recreation, family, and friends are in these days? How are you traveling to work? What is your home like? Don't exclude parts of your present life if they belong in your ideal days. Be as thorough as you can.

3. Set the description aside for at least a day. When you return, notice which details are most important to you. Which of them do you really long for? Make a list and decide which of them you wish to explore further.

4. What parts of these two ideal days are already in your life? Are there some aspects that could become part of your life without much difficulty? What changes could you make to bring that about?

END OF LIFE

In this practice, adapted from the Ignatian tradition of spiritual discernment, you learn about yourself and your values through a journey of the imagination.

1. Picture yourself being very old and in poor health. You might imagine yourself on your deathbed. You can think clearly, but you are very weak. You are with people who love you and care for you.

2. Look back over the story of your life. Consider the different parts of your life and what you have experienced. Ask yourself, "What is there that I really wish I had done/experienced/been?" Note what immediately comes to mind, writing it down if you wish.

3. Someone very close to you is beside your bed. You are asked if there is anything that you would like to have in your obituary besides the names of relatives and the jobs you've held—anything you'd like to be

remembered for. What have you stood for that means a great deal to you? You appreciate the question and respond. Write down your answer if you wish.

4. Take a few more minutes in this end-of-life imagining. Does any other wisdom surface for you? Then take a deep breath and return to who you are now, being aware of your body, mind, and spirit in the present.

5. What have you discovered about yourself? Did anything surprise you? Did anything show you what is truly important to you?

BEING CALLED—TWO PRACTICES

Passion, yearning, longing, calling: They all capture the mystery of feeling powerfully drawn to something more. These two practices invite you to listen closely to what might be calling you now.

People You Admire

1. Reflect on someone you have known personally whom you have greatly admired. What draws you to her? Then reflect on a person you greatly admire but don't know personally. What is it about this person that you especially admire?

2. You may be drawn to particular people because you recognize that their lives have a truth relevant to yours. Are you called to live out through your own life some aspect of these lives that you admire? If so, how?

Causes You Embrace

1. What causes or values do you hold most dear? Which ones stir something within you? Name them even if you have not lived them out as much as you wish to.

2. List your top five or ten values or causes for this stage of your life. Reflect on how they stir you. How are they part of your life? How do they serve as touchstones that guide your decisions?

PRACTICING WILLINGNESS

This meditative practice returns you to willingness, the foundation of spiritual decision making. Making this practice a daily habit helps to ground you in willingness and strengthens the place in you from which clarity for decisions can emerge.

1. Sit comfortably in a quiet place. Become aware of your willingness to open to the Spirit and receive guidance. Allow your body to express that willingness in some way, perhaps by opening your hands.
2. Open yourself to the Spirit with words like these (or others that are right for you): "Loving God, here I am. I want to see my way with your Light." Repeat these words or a phrase from them if you wish.
3. Your thoughts may wander, but bring them back repeatedly to remembering your willingness and openness. Let the words that declare your openness to the Spirit bring you back by repeating them again and again, as often as you need.
4. Sit quietly for fifteen minutes or longer in this practice.

NOTICING GOD'S NUDGES

Dig deep ... carefully cast forth the loose matter and get down to the rock, the sure foundation, and there hearken to the Divine Voice which gives a clear and certain sound.

—The Journal and Major
Essays of John Woolman

On Sunday mornings, I participate in silent Quaker worship. One by one we gather in the room with the benches facing into the center from all four sides. We sit together in silence, bringing into this time our clear intention to be open to the Spirit. Occasionally, someone will stand and say a few sentences, a "message" that invites our reflection. Then we return to silence.

Quaker worship provides an admirable structure for my own deepened listening. In order to discern the way forward, having a way of listening deeply is essential for all of us. We need to set aside space and time to go inside ourselves to listen for the truth we will find there. Whether we call it God's "nudge" or our own deep truth, we can't find the way forward unless we provide a space for the truth to rise into our awareness.

This is open listening, a listening with the intention of receiving whatever comes. Our open receptivity prepares us for a nudge from the Spirit. It is expectant listening. We let go of expectations for the specifics of what we should experience, but we come with the expectation that something will happen. And something does happen when we're quiet and waiting, even if we can't exactly name it. We might come without an agenda or come with a specific concern. We will receive a fresh perspective, a new insight, a conclusion, or perhaps an understanding that turns all previous thoughts upside down.

In Quaker worship, I come with the intention of being with others in silence for an hour. Being with the community affirms my intention to quietly listen and strengthens my attentiveness. But even with others, it is easy to appear quiet while I'm mentally jumping all around. Buddhism calls this "monkey mind," swinging from branch to branch, from thought to thought, not resting anywhere long enough to experience the tree itself. The benefit of the whole hour and the presence of others is that, eventually, the monkey in my mind settles down on one branch and is ready to listen.

Thus far, we've focused *attentiveness* on actively paying attention and noticing all that we can discover about ourselves, our inner lives, and our circumstances. This chapter focuses on the central importance of noticing the activity of the Spirit in our lives. God is always present to aid our discerning, but sometimes we are mysteriously nudged by God far beyond what our own seeking reveals to us. It may be a synchronicity or an unexpected invitation. Sometimes the nudge is more like a hearty shove. A door opens or closes, and we feel the movement of the Spirit in our lives.

"Discernment," writer Patricia Loring says in *Listening Spirituality: Personal Spiritual Practices Among Friends*, "is a gift from God, not a personal achievement." Spiritual discernment is about listening attentively so we can discover which of the possible paths for our lives are in keeping with God's ways, which decisions bring us into more harmonious alignment with the Divine. When we engage in deepened listening, what we are really listening for is the music of the Creator so we can live in better harmony with that music, so we can live within that music.

Spaces for stillness and reflection are often not easy to come by in modern life. But in the midst of decision making, we particularly need a spaciousness for reflection. As you think about your life, consider how you can create this kind of space. Can you reflect while you walk or exercise? What about taking a weekend away at a retreat house? Can you give yourself a leisurely, open-ended time for journaling, a spaciousness of time? Where are there possibilities for deepened listening in your life?

GOD DREAMED US INTO BEING

The Jewish philosopher and scholar of Jewish mystical traditions Martin Buber relates the following story in his *Tales of the Hasidim*. The Hasidic sage Rabbi Susya once said to a companion, "When I reach the next world, God will not ask me, 'Why were you not Moses?' God will ask me, 'Why were you not Rabbi Susya? Why were you not the person I created you to be?'"

Some years ago my friend Marc had a job that took him from school to school, presenting and selling educational games, toys, and books to teachers and to interested families. He felt good about the products he was selling, but he wasn't altogether satisfied with his life. One day at a school where he was doing his usual presentation, he met a Russian immigrant family and listened in fascination to their story of crossing the Atlantic, of taking a leap of faith to build a new life in an unknown land. As he drove away from the school, he suddenly knew he wanted to listen to people's stories much more than he wanted to sell them things. With tears, he knew it was time for his own leap of faith. He remembers how strongly he felt God's presence assuring him, "I love you, I am with you. Yes, this is what it looks like to be you." He left his job and entered graduate school to become a clinical social worker. He knew it was essential to have work where "I can be Marc." "What I do," he reflected, "needs to flow

out of who I am." Not Moses, not Rabbi Susya, but Marc. The fit
would be best when it flowed most naturally from his true,
authentic self.

Marcia came to parish ministry as a second career, though
she had long yearned for this work. It had called her since childhood, and finally she was serving a congregation. The difficulty
began for her when she discovered how much she still had to
learn. She grew anxious and began to question herself: "Who am
I to preach when I'm so awkward in the pulpit, to counsel others
when I'm so confused about myself?" When we met, she talked
about her paralyzing fear that she was going to fail, and she wondered why she ever thought she could be a minister.

When I asked Marcia why she had always wanted to be a
pastor, she sat in silence for a long time. Then she said, "I love the
people of the church. People need a spiritual community for their
Christian life, and my call is to serve it." She had remembered
why she was doing what she was doing. As crucial as the tasks of
ministry were, her ministry was grounded in *who* she was, not
what she did. And at the heart of who she was lay the desire to
love and serve others in the community. In time, she grew more
at ease with pastoral care and sermon delivery, but she continued
to remember that the center of her ministry was her unique self,
not the functions she fulfilled.

The word *authentic* comes from the ancient Greek *authen-
tikos,* meaning "genuine" or "original." Something authentic has
the authority (the authorship) of its original creator. While the
meaning of *authentic* has changed little through the centuries, I
believe an essential nuance has slipped away. We need to reclaim
authenticity as living out of the authority of our Creator. Our
authenticity is grounded in God, who with infinite imagination
and inventiveness is dreaming each of us into a unique and original being: "Oh, yes, this one is shaped for community life, since
she can both lead and lovingly tend to others. She has a passion
for truthful speaking and a depth of intellectual understanding.

Perhaps she'll be a teacher, or maybe a minister. Or perhaps she'll find another path to live out her authentic self."

In his poem "As Kingfishers Catch Fire," Gerard Manley Hopkins captures the meaning of *authenticity* when he writes about the force within each creature to pour forth its uniqueness:

> Each mortal thing does one thing and the same:
> Deals out that being indoors each one dwells;
> Selves—goes itself; *myself* it speaks and spells;
> Crying *What I do is me: for that I came.*

A kingfisher is genetically engineered to know what its life is about. For us, it's more challenging. What authentic truth of our being shapes our lives? To what deep truth can we give ourselves? What kind of presence in the world is uniquely ours? There is something deep within each of us that *knows* who we are and what we are called to live for.

When Rabbi Susya, Marc, or Marcia make decisions grounded in their authentic selves, these decisions arise from what psychologist Carl Jung called the true self, who we *truly* are. This is the person God dreamed of us being, the one we've been created to be. Marc said, "I don't know who I truly am, so I need God to show me who I truly am." Listening deeply, we can discover more and more who we truly are. When we live most fully *who* we are created to be, *what* we do takes its proper place. This means we acknowledge the Creator's authorship and align ourselves with a God of love in the uniqueness of ourselves. Which path we finally choose is of less importance than that alignment.

In *An Altar in the World,* preacher and writer Barbara Brown Taylor recounts her struggles to find the vocational path that was right for her. There were so many roads she could travel and no clear guide as to which she should choose. She was determined to wrestle an answer from God, and, night after night, she climbed the rickety fire escape of a graduate school building to be alone and listen. Frightened of the height and her precarious perch, she still persisted. Finally, she recounts, there was an answer. "Do anything that pleases you," she heard, "and belong to me."

I described the importance of listening earlier in this chapter. To draw our decisions from our authorship in God, we need to give time and space to listening. We need to pay attention to the deepest truths within us. We need to ask ourselves, "If I make this decision based on the best and truest self I am, based on the person God dreamed me to be, how will I decide?" And then we wait, listening for the truth to come.

Barbara Brown Taylor still needed to make specific decisions for her life, just as we still need to make specific decisions for our lives. However, by acknowledging that we belong to the great Author, our grounding in God casts the whole situation in a new light. It frees us to create our lives with God, knowing that we have God's loving companionship on the path we choose, no matter which decision we make.

God's Timing

Deepening our listening and growing into greater authenticity are both essential for the discernment process, but sometimes it seems that the most vital factor in our decisions is timing. We're creatures of time, of hours and days and years, which pass with increasing speed. Is this the right time? When is it my turn? Should I wait? How will I know when to proceed?

Often the timing of decisions is determined for us. Educational institutions have deadlines. Job openings come, and then they're gone. Even parenthood has its biological clock. Sometimes we may need to make a choice when we don't like the options. Who hasn't been caught in that kind of forced-choice situation?

Just as there are multiple "right" paths, there are multiple "so-so" paths. We may need to choose a path that seems only half-right. When we are pushed to make a decision before we are ready, or when no decision seems like the right one, we must remember the Spirit's presence as we make the next decisions on the path. Living into the decisions we've made is always about making more decisions, and many of our decisions are actually about how to walk the path. *How* we walk the path is as important as which path we take. Listening to the Spirit and paying attention to God's nudges will continue to guide our steps.

At other times our decision making has no external deadline forcing us to make a choice. The big *what, when,* and *if* questions we struggle with can go on for a very long time. Then God's nudges may be the gift that tells us when the time is right.

Sometimes when there seems no way forward for a heartfelt desire, the nudge from God is to wait. The door is closed; perhaps it always will be closed or perhaps it will open in the future. Connie had been adopted as a baby into a wonderful and loving family. As an adult, she yearned to give back, offering something from her own story to families who were adopting. She knew she had something of importance to give, but the adoption agency she contacted wasn't interested in working with her in the way she envisioned. They invited her to be a board member, but she knew her calling was to serve adoptive parents. Reluctantly, she set aside the dream and focused on her work and her growing family.

A few years passed, and Connie's children grew up and left home. It was a new stage of her life. "I felt an urgency in my spirit," she says. "I had a sense that this was the right time." She called the adoption agency again. This time they welcomed her presence and her support of adoptive parents with open arms. She could volunteer as a teacher of adoption classes. She could tell of her experience as an adopted child. They needed her, and they needed her now.

As Connie reflected on her story, she realized that her first inquiry to the adoption agency didn't fit her life at that time. She wasn't ready for a large volunteer investment. But the longing to serve others by sharing her story was God's nudge, and it persisted. We can often recognize God's nudges by their persistence over time.

An experience of God's timing came to me several years ago as a vote of approval, an affirmation of a difficult decision I'd already made. With agonizing carefulness, I had decided to study for a term at Pendle Hill, the Quaker center for study and contemplation near Philadelphia, leaving my home and my husband for an adventure into the unknown. The final clarity for this decision came just after I'd met with a committee of friends who had gathered to listen with me for God's guidance in this decision.

Early the next morning I received a call from the admissions director at Pendle Hill. She wondered if I had ever considered coming to study there, saying that my name appeared on a list of possible students that had sat on her desk for several months. Since only my husband knew of the decision I'd made the evening before, this call was an extraordinary affirmation. Whatever the future would hold, I felt the blessing of a mysterious "Yes! Go for it" from God.

Messages from God come in many shapes and forms. While we may be awed at the synchronicities described above, there are many smaller invitations that come as we pay attention. God's nudges can come through simply noticing something about ourselves (I love to work with my hands) or a dream (I dream of living abroad) or perhaps even a discomfort (the uneasiness of holding a grudge).

WHEN EGOS ARE INVOLVED

Spiritual discernment is made harder because our egos quickly want to become the center of attention. When we want to listen deeply for wisdom beyond our own, trying to hear the invitation to live more authentically, the ego pops up all too often, convinced that it's all about *me, me, me.*

Having a sense of self is essential to healthy human life. A sense of identity gives us an understanding of who we are, especially in terms of relatively stable characteristics, such as personality or skills, which we examined in chapter 3. The ego is the part of our identity that needs to keep on establishing who we are. It needs to keep on proving itself or proclaiming itself. The ego interprets everything that happens in light of its own needs— for approval and validation, acceptance and success. There is a significant difference between feeling swayed to make a particular choice by the ego's anxiety or pride and feeling the freedom of the real and authentic inner self opening the way.

Last autumn I hiked with a group of friends in some of the remoter canyons of southern Utah. We had two leaders and each day we could choose between a moderate and a challenging hike. Most people chose the moderate one because it was just as beautiful and not as exhausting. I knew I wasn't in great physical shape, but I always chose the challenging one. I had something to prove. I wanted to show that, despite being one of the older hikers, I could still do it! Certainly there was nothing wrong with choosing the challenging hike, even to test my limits. Yet what I noticed as I panted along the trail was that I wasn't completely free to choose the hike that would bring me the most pleasure. My ego insisted that I choose the challenging hike because it needed to show off both my determination and my physical fitness.

Discernment is the ability to make distinctions, being able to distinguish between those impulses that come from ego needs and those that arise from the authentic, true self. A test of whether the authentic, true self or the ego is in the driver's seat is how much freedom we feel in making the decision. If I had freely chosen my hike of the day, I might have chosen the moderate hike some days. The difference lay in the insistence of my ego, its anxiety that I show what I could do. Can we identify the anxiety or sense of self-conscious pride that the ego brings to a situation? Can we discriminate between the times when the ego limits our freedom to choose the path and when we are free?

When Alex wanted to build a sunroom on to his house, he planned to do it himself over weekends and long summer evenings. He knew construction, and had designed the room his family had always wanted. But the summer softball league took many evenings, and weekends in the mountains took more time. Nevertheless, he was determined that this would be his project; he knew he could do it, and he kept talking about how it would look when it was finished. Unfortunately, when October arrived, only the foundation was built and he knew that the sunroom wouldn't be completed until next year. As he thought about where the summer had gone, he realized that he had insisted he would build the sunroom because pride in *his* project wouldn't let him admit that he needed more help and more time than he had. Next summer, he decided, he wouldn't try to prove anything—he'd hire some help and simply get it done.

Reflect for a minute on a decision you need to make. When you consider the possible choices for your decision, how free are you to choose the one that is most right for you? Do you sense your ego nudging you toward one option? Can you identify *why* you are being pushed in that direction?

Distinguishing between the ego's nudges and God's nudges is always a challenge because they do overlap. Anything the Spirit nudges us to be or do can be taken on by the ego (if it increases our importance) or fought against by the ego (if it diminishes our personal importance or status). The Spirit nudges us toward being more authentic, growing more into our true self. Ego is fine with that process—as long as it leads to success or approval!

When we find ourselves in this predicament, we need to return again to our sense of *willingness*. Can we let ourselves be open to what the Light shows us and move forward in trust, not knowing whether that will lead to the kind of success the ego recognizes? Can we remember that allowing the Spirit to shape the path brings deeper fulfillment and greater freedom than the search for success and approval can ever give? The ego does play a significant role in our lives. It helps us know who we are; it helps us establish a sense of identity. But, as Franciscan priest Richard Rohr says in *Everything Belongs,* "The only problem is that our culture teaches that ego is the only game in town." Fortunately, we know there is another game in town.

In Mother Teresa's words, "We are called by God to be faithful, not successful." Being faithful means taking the risk of being open and attentive to God's nudges. It means deeply listening to how much of the ego underlies any impulse or yearning and how much comes from a deeper source that pulls us toward authenticity. Though nudges from our egos and nudges from the Spirit may look the same on the outside, or even lead to the same outcome, it matters greatly within us which one finally guides our decision making.

Practices for Finding Your Way

These practices help us to deepen our awareness of God's presence and activity in our lives. There are many ways to be attentive to God's presence and activity, so you can adapt these practices to fit the situation of your life. Create your own practices of attentiveness!

DEEPENED LISTENING

In this practice, you are giving yourself space in which to listen deeply and attend to the Spirit. New insights may come, but your purpose is to be fully present to your life and open to God. I suggest an hour as a minimum, but you could incorporate it into a retreat of a day or more.

1. Find a physical setting that helps you quiet your mind. You may find that sounds are less of a distraction than activities going on around you that pull your thoughts away from your intention for this time.

You might dedicate your daily walk to attentiveness to God, or you might sit quietly in solitude.

2. Acknowledge your intention to be open to whatever may come to you. Offer this time to God. You might say the words of your intention: "Here I am, willing to receive whatever understanding comes." Or you might say, "I give this time to being open to the Spirit." Perhaps one word or a gesture will express your intention. You might light a candle if you are sitting, or hold some small special object (a stone, a seashell, prayer beads) in your hands.

3. Allow your mind to wander freely. The purpose of the practice is not to solve a problem or discover an answer but to be open to God. This provides the fertile ground from which new understandings and new insights can grow. You could ask yourself, "How is God present in this part of my life? Or in this part?" If new understandings come, hold them lightly, with gratitude.

4. Keep returning to your intention for this time, remembering your desire to dedicate it to being open to God. Perhaps you will repeatedly say the words of intention or offer the gesture of opening to God.

5. When the time is drawing to an end, when the hour, the walk, or the retreat is just about over, acknowledge your gratitude with a few prayerful words. Be aware of how your body and spirit have been nurtured through this spacious experience.

EXAMEN FOR GOD'S INVITATIONS

The ancient prayer of *examen* is a review of the day just past, a look at how God's loving presence has been with you during the day. This form of the *examen* looks at

God's nudges or invitations throughout the day. You may want to write about this in a journal, or you may find it easier to do this practice when you are already in bed and on the way to sleep.

1. Quiet yourself and gently look back over your day. You are not judging the day or yourself, simply observing what it was like, and preparing to let go of it.

2. Ask yourself: Where did I notice God's invitations for my life today? While some invitations or nudges are powerful, others may be small urges to do a kindly deed or reach out to another in some way. Perhaps the nudge was a sudden desire to "stop and smell the roses," to pause and notice something beautiful. Take your time and review your day for any invitation you recall.

3. Ask yourself: How did I respond to God's invitations in my life today? Again, the response may have been something small, like a friendly gesture at the check-out line in the supermarket. You may also notice that you ignored some of God's nudges. What did you ignore and what does that mean to you?

4. With a gesture of release, let go of the day, offering it to the God of love. Acknowledge your gratitude for the nudges you have received and express your desire to be open and responsive to them tomorrow.

LIVING AUTHENTICALLY

This journaling practice explores what we know about how it feels to live out of our true self, with an authenticity grounded in the Spirit, as well as what it is like to be inauthentic. While our lives are always a mix of the two, naming what it is like to live as the true self helps steer us toward authenticity.

1. Think back on a situation in which you felt you were as wholly and fully yourself as you've ever been. What do you remember about that experience? How did it feel? What signs within and around you confirmed your sense of authenticity?
2. Then recall a situation in which you felt that you were being false to yourself, and acting in a way that wasn't truly who you are. What do you remember most about that situation, and how did it feel? What signs indicated to you that you were not being true to yourself?
3. Now compare the two accounts you have written. What do you notice about the two situations—their similarities and differences? How can these observations help you in your daily life? How can they help you make decisions?

THE HABIT OF ATTENTIVENESS

People usually consider walking on water or in thin air a miracle. But I think the real miracle is not to walk either on water or in thin air but to walk on earth.
—*Thich Nhat Hanh,* The Miracle of Mindfulness

A friend once told me the story of how she decided to handle a difficult relationship with a coworker with whom she had been struggling for years over their shared supervisory responsibilities. "I knew that I needed to ask for mediation, for a session with her and a trained mediator," she said.

"What amazed me," she added, "is that I didn't become clear about what to do when I was trying to figure it out, but rather when I was quietly sitting on my deck. I was focusing on my breathing and simply being attentive to what I saw and heard in the present moment. I discovered that being in the now is the only way to get where you need to go."

As this example shows, *attentiveness* can help us reach clarity in decisions when we least expect it. But it is far more than a tool for making decisions. It is a policy for living, a practice for life that can transform our days. The miracle of walking on earth attentively, or "mindfully," as Buddhist monk Thich Nhat Hanh says, makes us come alive in a new way. We notice the ordinary and find it extraordinary. We experience the extraordinary and find ourselves part of the miracle of being.

BEING AWAKE

Buddha is a Sanskrit word meaning "one who is awake." The story is told that once the Buddha met someone on the road who, impressed by his peaceful radiance, stopped him and asked, "Who are you? Are you a god? A magician?" "No," replied the quiet monk with the mysterious half-smile. "Are you even a *man*?" his questioner asked. And the Buddha replied serenely, "I am awake."

I have often wondered what it is like to be fully awake. I know I am generally half-awake at best. How awake are you? Without habits of attentiveness, we tend to live on autopilot, depending on our fixed routines and past patterns to get us through the day. Attentiveness wakes us up. The more attentive we are, the more we begin to inhabit our lives rather than just sleepwalk through them.

In summertime, my husband, Larry, and I give lots of attention to our garden. As we work, we are surrounded by trees and green grass, flowers tumbling down the hillside, bushes drooping and colorful with raspberries or blueberries, apple trees, peach trees, and vegetables ripening into their varied shapes and colors. Lavender and roses perfume the air and birds swoop from their bath among the herbs to their nests hidden in the pines. Insects of all types buzz and flap and jump and crawl. Each day brings something new to notice.

Through the years that we have been fellow gardeners, Larry and I have gradually developed our own specialties. He notices the berries (How close to ripeness are they? Have the Japanese beetles begun their annual attack?), while I tend the tomatoes, beans, zucchini, and weeds (How can they grow so fast?). He sees that the grass is growing patchily, while I, walking on that same patchy grass, focus on the first dahlia opening and the renewal of the deep blue campanula. We have directed our attentiveness and we don't see the whole garden. Unless he points it out, I don't notice the health of the berries. Unless I show him, he doesn't notice the blooming clematis partly hidden within the climbing roses.

But sometimes we walk the garden together. Hand in hand at the end of the day, we show each other what we've noticed, and together we look at the whole garden. We bring to this walk an open attention very different from our usual task-focused attention. We notice whatever there is to see; our only purpose is to be attentive to what is there. We are awake to the whole garden.

Being awake to the whole garden, or to the whole tapestry of our lives, constitutes open attentiveness. Focused attention is important to accomplish tasks, whether in the garden or on the computer, in the automobile or in the household. But to be fully alive, we need to practice open attentiveness, too. When I walk out the door, not only to check the water in the birdbath, but also to see whatever there is to see, I am more awake. I approach the world knowing there *is* more to notice, and I expect to be surprised. I see as if all were fresh to my eyes. Can we remember to be awake? Can we bring fresh vision to whatever we might notice?

French philosopher and mystic Simone Weil wrote in *Waiting for God,* "Absolutely unmixed attention is prayer." When we really attend to the world around us and the life we're living, we open to the Presence, to the sacred Spirit that is all around us in the world. Words are not necessary for praying, but I may murmur a simple "wow" prayer as I realize the intricacy of the butterfly wing or the sky-enlarging magnificence of a winter sunset. If I'm truly attentive to the small kindness of the stranger who warmly smiled as she opened the door for me, when we both were carrying heavy burdens, I may whisper a "thank you" prayer.

Awake to Ordinary Uniqueness

After a heavy snowfall a few winters ago, I looked out my kitchen window and saw my eighty-year-old neighbor shoveling her driveway. Ruth is a strong and independent woman who usually takes weather in her stride, but this was a hard, cold winter, so she welcomed my offer of help. As we worked, we enjoyed sharing our news. I listened to stories of her friends who lived in Peru and I told her how my daughters were faring in college. When the driveway was cleared by the middle of the afternoon, Ruth invited me into her house to warm up, and we continued visiting over her homemade shoofly pie and a cup of coffee. I commented on the new color of her kitchen and she told me about her plans to visit her cousins after the weather cleared up.

Then, suddenly, I "woke up." It was all very ordinary, but I suddenly woke up and really saw her, and the whole room lit up. The day put on a glow not entirely explained by neighborly friendship and the tingle of my warming toes. I saw Ruth more clearly, her curly white hair, her slippered feet padding around in her kitchen, her talking about how she'd grown to depend on her microwave. This was Ruth, a never-to-be-repeated human being. I attended to the particularity of my neighbor, not any generic neighbor, but this unique one. I noticed the day, not an ordinary snowy day, but this one, a never-to-be-repeated day. And when I really tasted the shoofly pie, that marvelous Pennsylvania Dutch specialty, its smooth molasses-y flavor was superb.

I'd like to cultivate that state of being awake and aware every day. I'd like to see and appreciate the uniqueness of all the ordinary pieces of my days. I want to notice the tingle of the hot shower in the morning and the fragrant warmth of my daily cup of coffee. I'd like to be awake as I drive to work every day and as I chop carrots and onions for dinner in the evening.

It does not come easily but, even during our most ordinary days, it is possible to cultivate the fullness of being awake. When we are attentive to the work and to the day, we find the miracle of uniqueness that lies within each moment. Chinese monks of a thousand years ago knew this well. They found their spiritual practices in the ordinary activities of the day: chopping wood and carrying water. Their days were filled with simple, basic activities, as are ours. If they could turn repetitive hard work into spiritual practice, so can we. What kind of spiritual practices of attentiveness might be ours today? What might be our equivalent of chopping wood and carrying water? Checking e-mail and loading the dishwasher? Commuting to work and putting the children to bed?

Someone once told me that his spiritual practice was driving his daughters to school early every morning. He had made a conscious decision to be awake and attentive to them as they—and he—were beginning the day. He knew he had a tendency to slide into unawareness, making the commute on autopilot and finding his daughters' morning chatter easy to turn off, but he always returned to his desire to be aware of them and the uniqueness of the day they were starting together.

The key to this kind of attentiveness is *mindfulness*. Do what you are doing while you are doing it; be where you are while you are there. Thich Nhat Hanh's classic *Miracle of Mindfulness* teaches us how to eat an orange. Pay attention to the orange while we're eating it, he tells us. Peel it carefully and be aware of the fragrance. Notice its interior, and be conscious of its juicy smoothness and sweet flavor, the feel of it as we chew and while we swallow. It sounds very simple, but often we are distracted, eating the orange while mentally tilting forward into what comes next—"What should I do about the committee meeting tonight?"—or backward into whatever has just ended—"How could I have done that?" Or perhaps we're deeply engaged in conversation or watching television. Swallowing the last section comes as a surprise—we didn't even notice when we swallowed all the others.

Certainly loading the dishwasher and checking e-mail are very different from indulging in the sensory awareness of eating an orange. The experience of nature, like strolling in my garden, is deeply renewing, bringing a profound sense of aliveness and refreshment. Not all experiences make it so easy to be awake. But the same practice of noticing and being awake can enter all our activities. For example, as I write on my laptop, I focus on the words I am typing and the thoughts behind them. This is narrow, focused attention. It is necessary and important. But I need to pause in my work and become aware of it. Yes, this is what I am doing right now, at this moment. I notice the placement of my hands and the posture of my back. I look around, letting my eyes drift away from the computer screen. Perhaps I look out the window and see a cardinal with a tiny seed in its bill perched at the birdfeeder. I reconnect myself to where I am, sitting on my favorite cushion in my study with the laptop on my lap. I notice my cat sleeping under my desk and wonder how long he has been there. The gift of such pausing is in waking up, in a renewed aliveness. I may even notice the rhythm of my breath as it enters and leaves my body.

Take a moment to stop reading and just be aware. Notice the posture of your body and the feel of the book in your hands. Separate yourself from the words on the page and look around you. What do you see and hear? Notice something that you usually don't pay attention to—a lamp, a photograph, a small bowl, how the light is streaming through the window. If it's an object, reach out and touch it. What makes it unique?

BREATHE IN, BREATHE OUT

In *A Thomas Merton Reader,* Trappist monk, theologian, and poet Thomas Merton is quoted as saying, "What I wear is pants. What I do is live. How I pray is breathe." Breathing is the most ordinary of activities—and the essential one. All around the world, religious traditions focus on breathing as a spiritual practice. Sometimes how the breath flows is at the heart of the practice, but paying attention to breathing is always important. In Hebrew, the word *ruach* translates as both "breath" and "spirit," acknowledging the centrality of spirit in breathing. Sufi Muslims, Zen Buddhists, Jewish mystics, and meditating Christians all recognize the sacredness of breath and the importance of how we breathe.

Stop reading again and notice your breathing. While you were reading, you were breathing, so now notice your breath. Breathe in, breathe out. Does the rhythm of your breathing seem slow or quick? Are you breathing from your abdomen or is it mostly your chest that rises and falls? Take a really deep breath, opening and holding it briefly, then release it fully. How does that feel different? Can you picture the soft lungs within your chest expanding and then contracting? As you continue to read, you might pause at the end of this page to once again notice your breathing. Perhaps you will pause at the end of each page and notice that you are still breathing.

When we remember to pay attention to our breathing, we are more likely to notice and be awake to other sensations within and around us. We are more attentive to being alive. We may echo Merton and consider our breathing itself as a prayer. Conscious breathing, being attentive to our breathing, deepens the prayer.

PAUSING

We pause in the midst of activity all the time, but we usually call it "taking a break." We take a break from exercise and "catch our breath." (A revealing metaphor: I notice my breath because I'm "out of breath," but once I've caught it, I generally ignore it.) We take a lunch break, a coffee break, and a bathroom break. I propose that we take an "awareness break," a pause to reclaim the awareness of where we are, who we are, and what we're doing. It's an opportunity to wake up again.

What would an awareness break look like? I had just written this when my phone rang, a call from my two- and four-year-old granddaughters who live on the other side of the country. They love to make phone calls, and though it isn't easy to understand everything they say, I am always glad to hear their "I love you, Oma." This was a true awareness break, waking me up to my unique world and my grandmotherly place in it. But it was a break that came to me as an interruption, not one I chose. What would it look like to choose awareness breaks?

In the Benedictine monastic tradition, the bells called the monks to prayer eight times in the course of a twenty-four-hour day. Although today most Benedictine monasteries do not wake for vigils in the middle of the night, the daily times of prayer from matins in the morning to compline at night remain as central as they always have been. They provide an opportunity for the monks to recall who they are, where they are, what they're doing—and to remember why they're doing it. Such attentiveness brings them to prayer.

The Benedictine rhythm of life is shaped by these times of prayer and attentiveness. Although our lives don't have the same shape, they do offer opportunities for attentiveness if we look for them. We can create a habit of pausing so that it becomes a natural part of the rhythm of the day. We might follow the Benedictine practice of pausing for reflection at specific times of day, no matter what we are doing. That will give us a regular time for paying attention and remembering what is real, a time for noticing our breathing and our bodies. If we recognize that this is prayer, words may rise to our consciousness to express something from the moment, a need we have, or perhaps simple gratitude.

A natural way of weaving these opportunities throughout the day is to take a pause for awareness between the completion of one task or activity and the beginning of the next. A friend has created a habit of pausing that I admire. She works from home, and, after she completes one task, she moves to another room to sit in a particular chair for five minutes. During that time, she may center herself with a prayer. She may check in with her body, noticing her breathing or places of tension or tiredness. She limits herself to five minutes. This is not a coffee break, but an invitation to wake up to the present moment and her gratitude to be alive in it.

There are all kinds of possibilities. Perhaps you arrive home only to immediately start in on your computer. Could you pause on the threshold instead, and take a few moments to center your-self? Do you have family members and pets to greet? Can you stand in front of a window and look out, simply breathing and waking up to where you are? Can you walk through the space, noticing what is beautiful in your home? Through this mindful transition, you will ground yourself in your home, and in your own being as well.

Sometimes pauses at home or work may seem impossible. At home the children are clamoring for attention, dinner needs to be made, and the dog wants to go out. Workplaces may be public; looking out the window for five minutes is definitely not encouraged. But you can get up and stretch—a pause need only be as long as a breath if you do it in full awareness of your breathing and your stretching. It may help to have a word or phrase, or perhaps an affirmation or prayer, to silently repeat as you breathe. Phrases such as "God, I am here, You are here" or "I am breathing" or "Now, here, peace" can sink in and pro-vide true refreshment in the middle of a stressful day.

The attention to breathing and the phrase to repeat can both be supported by touch. A small stone or shell from a relaxing vaca-tion, a *mezuzah* on the doorway at home, a picture of a loved one all call forth another sensory experience, inviting us to recollect ourselves, to remember who we are in the midst of the pressure and busyness that unbalance us and make us forget.

At home the presence of the children, the dog, the dinner, and the laundry can be equally unbalancing. What reminders can recall us to who we are and where we are? Perhaps our attention seems so drawn into the turmoil around us that reflecting with a phrase and some conscious breathing in the middle of it all simply doesn't seem possible. When I was a frazzled mother of young children, with dinner to prepare and laundry to do after coming home from work, pausing was probably the furthest thing from my mind. I dreamed of running away, maybe, but not pausing and becoming more attentive to what was right in front of me. But that is the invitation: When you can't run away, go further in. Change the way you are in it. The attentiveness might need to be within the turmoil itself. To remember the uniqueness of these children, this food, or even that pile of dirty laundry is to see and to live in the present moment. As I look at these children, see this pasta, check this shirt for dirt, I reclaim my life and being once again.

Slowing the pace of busyness helps us become attentive to the specificity of our lives. A brief time of slowing down can make all the difference. Even when I am doing many things at once, I can stop and breathe for a moment with my hands on the pile of dirty laundry, conscious of the children and the TV and the pasta. Furthermore, I can deliberately choose to move more slowly at times like these. A meditation exercise called "slow walking" allows practitioners to become more attentive to what is around and within them. Perhaps a time of slow laundry sorting would work just as well. Someone told me once that doing laundry was his own private time for praying for each family member who would wear the clothing. What pace of food preparation and eating helps us become attentive to the gift of sustenance? What pace of interaction with family fosters awareness of each one's uniqueness and your relationship with them?

DISCERNMENT FOR DAILY LIVING THROUGH DAILY NOTICING

We began this chapter by observing that being in the now, in the present, is the only way to get where we need to go. Being present and aware provides space for fresh clarity to arise for ordinary, daily decisions as well as for large, life-changing ones. A daily habit of attentiveness not only helps us to be awake and more fully alive but also helps us make the everyday decisions of our lives.

After all, small decisions remain a constant in our lives, and our habits of noticing help us make our way through them. On the simplest level, if I've noticed that there is no milk in my refrigerator, I'd much rather buy some on the way home from work than make an extra trip to the store. If I am attentive to my body and notice extra lethargy as the workday closes, I can choose my evening's activities carefully and decide whether a stop at the gym would be refreshing, or whether heading for bed as soon as the children are tucked in would be the better option.

The daily habit of attentiveness smooths out my relationships. When I see that a coworker is struggling, perhaps withdrawn or surreptitiously wiping away tears, my noticing helps shape my interactions with her. I choose to be gentler and more patient and perhaps ask about her distress. When I pay attention to my impulse to say or do something hurtful to another, I can choose to harness the impulse. If I am irritated by the way my friend is always late for our dates, I need to notice that I'm irritated. Then I can consider how to speak in a way that preserves our friendship. If I don't acknowledge my irritation, I am more likely to blurt out something I later wish had been left unsaid.

Like minor steering adjustments when driving a car, these small, ordinary decisions help us steer our lives to avoid accidents. Small adjustments to straighten us out and keep us on the road are constantly necessary, no matter how straight the street. As I reflect on the day just past, my "steering" decisions include how I greeted my husband as he arrived home from work. I noticed that he was feeling low, so I chose to greet him warmly and ask him what was bothering him. His sharing about the stress of his day led us to a thoughtful conversation about the shape of our work lives in the future, which drew us closer to each other.

The practice of attentiveness is needed in steering both our cars and our lives. Small, daily decisions are as important in living as the large decisions. The big decisions, such as where to live or what career to pursue, may actually be less important to a fulfilled, contented life than the small daily decisions on how to respond to irritations that come our way.

Daily awareness inevitably leads to gratitude. When we pay attention to what is present in our lives, we have a chance to claim as blessings those ordinary things we usually overlook. In his book *Gratefulness, the Heart of Prayer,* Brother David Steindl-Rast calls such noticing a "wonderment." We pause and notice the daily, ordinary blessings, and they are fresh. We respond with wonder and gratitude.

My breath, which I only notice when I need to catch it, is a blessing. The warmth of a coat on a winter's day and the warmth of balmy breezes in summertime, the exquisite variety of tastes in my mouth and the equally exquisite variety of music in my ear, the snuggle of a child in my arms and the softness of a dandelion blossom—all are blessings that fill me with the gladness of gratitude.

A story from Jewish tradition says that on the day of judgment God will ask one question of each of us. Perhaps a bit wistfully, the Divine One will ask, "Did you enjoy my world?" Do we notice it sufficiently to respond, "Oh, yes!"?

Practices for Finding Your Way

Practices for everyday attentiveness invite us to be creative. While this chapter and the exercises described here may be helpful, it is important to shape your daily awareness so that it fits *your* days. Every life has some space for attentiveness. Where is your space?

LECTIO DIVINA IN THE WORLD OF NATURE

Lectio divina is the spiritual practice of reading sacred writings slowly and prayerfully, and then meditating on them. It calls for an attentiveness to the words and how they speak uniquely to each person. In the practice below, you will learn to "read" what the Celtic Christian tradition calls "God's other book," the natural world.

1. Begin this experience outdoors by standing or sitting completely still. Offer this time to God and consciously open yourself, willing to see or hear or feel whatever may come your way. Acknowledge that you have no goal to achieve. You simply want to notice what is in front of you and be open to God's presence.
2. Look around and observe. Use all your senses. You might slowly begin to walk. If something seems to pull your attention, go with it; carefully observe it and experience it. It may be a cloud, an insect, a plant growing close by.
3. Spend more time with it than you think you need to. Is there some way it is speaking to you? Is there any reflection about your life that arises as you study it? For example, you may notice that the shapes of various trees and their straightness or roundness or missing branches invite you to reflect on various aspects of your life. Or you may notice a stone whose pattern or shape speaks to you of your life.

4. Continue walking as long as you wish, expecting that something will stop you, and that you will allow it to speak to you.

PRACTICES FOR PAUSING

This practice particularly lends itself to being creative. I list some possibilities for pausing, but you need to discover the opportunities in your own life. To form the *habit* of pausing is more challenging than discovering the right time and space for it. It can be helpful to have a friend who is also learning to pause and be attentive, since accountability will strengthen the habit.

1. Explore possibilities for brief "awareness breaks" in your day. Examples:

   - Write "awareness break" or "appointment with God" in your appointment book at specific hours.
   - The enforced idleness of traffic stoplights.
   - Time in the shower or the bath.
   - Set a timer every few hours to remind you; electronic aids are very helpful!
   - Anywhere you are forced to wait (an appointment, a slow Internet connection, heating something in the microwave).
   - In your car before you start it or before you leave it.
   - When your child wakes you up at night.
   - When you pass the same billboard every day on your way to work.

2. When you have given yourself a pause, take note of your body—its position and comfort level. Notice your breathing, and take a few deep breaths to stretch your chest. Notice what messages your senses are sending you. What are you seeing, hearing, feeling on your skin, touching, or smelling?

3. Remember who you are. Recollect those parts of yourself that you may not have been remembering just before the pause. Name yourself as a child of God or as one who is loved by God, or create a name that will connect you to the Spirit in any way that is right for you.

4. Stay with this pause as long you can. When you reenter your activity, begin slowly; be consciously aware of what you are doing.

CULTIVATING GRATITUDE

This is a practice that is never finished. Without cultivating gratitude, we may notice whatever is *not* blessing our lives without giving attention to everything that *is* blessing us. Here are two ways of remembering those parts of our lives for which we feel gratitude.

Prayer Beads

A circle or string of beads can help you focus your gratitude. While it can be especially meaningful to have prayer beads from a religious tradition, any beads strung together will become prayer beads as you use them. Create your own if you wish. While traditional prayer-bead circles have large numbers of beads (50 in a Catholic rosary, 99 in an Islamic prayer strand, and 108 in Buddhist and Hindu traditions), having fewer beads provides an endless circle for gratitude just as well.

1. Holding the beads in your hands, pause for a moment in awareness of your life's blessedness.

2. With your fingers touching one bead, name a specific aspect of your life—a person, a situation, something physical or emotional, or anything at all for which you feel gladness and gratitude. Pause for a moment to let yourself feel the gratitude, and then

go on to the next, naming another source of gratitude in your life.

3. Continue moving from bead to bead around the circle, or going back and forth on a line of beads. You
will not run out of things to feel grateful for, no matter how much hardship, pain, and grief are also in
your life. At the end, hold all the beads cupped in
your hand in gratitude for all that is good.

Gratitude Journal

For some people, writing may be the best way of noticing what you are grateful for. You may want to designate
a "gratitude journal" and add to it daily, or build this
practice into every journaling experience.

1. Ask yourself, "What am I grateful for today?" and
begin writing. You could make a list or describe in
great detail what you are grateful for.
2. Revisit your gratitude journal when you have lost your
sense of gratitude. Add to it regularly. Repeat yourself freely, reminding yourself of ongoing blessings.

REMEMBERING AND RELEASING THE DAY

The close of the day is a good time to be attentive and
remember the experiences of the day. This practice,
grounded in the Ignatian *examen* prayer, suggests a few
questions to guide your reflection. The purpose is not to
judge the day or yourself, but simply to acknowledge it
and release it. (See also the practice on pages 92–93,
"*Examen* for God's Invitations.")

1. Set aside a quiet time toward the end of your day to
look back over it. Ask yourself, "What was life-giving
in this day?" and take some time to remember what
brought you life (or gladness or fulfillment). Then ask

yourself, "What was life-draining about this day?" and remember what drained you.

2. An alternative set of questions could be "Where did I notice God's love today?" and "Where did I receive God's love and give God's love today?" Or you could consider "When was I really awake today?" and "When was I just drifting, not awake at all?"

3. Spend as much time with the questions as is right for you. Then, perhaps with a gesture of release, let go of the day, offering it to a loving God.

Here we are, Loving One, Light
toward whom our faces turn.

You are the Dancer and
we would learn to dance with you,
a dance of grace and of truth,
of love and of wisdom,
a dance of life.

We would learn to dance,
how to step, how to pause,
how to weave among the others
responding to your music
through the dance of life.

And even when
we forget the steps and fumble,
forget the pause and lose our place,
forget the other dancers, and collide,
we still want to continue
to learn the dance.

Longing to respond with ready faithfulness
yet struggling to trust
the weaving of the dance,
needing gentle touch to steady us,
needing Light to show the way,

Here we are, Loving One, ready to begin.

PART III

RESPONSIVENESS

TESTING OUR DECISIONS

The outer distractions of our interests reflect an inner lack of integration of our own lives. We are trying to be several selves at once, without all our selves being organized by a single, mastering Life within us. Each of us tends to be, not a single self, but a whole committee of selves.

—*Thomas Kelly,* A Testament of Devotion

In the Quaker tradition, decisions are not made by voting. Rather, decisions are made by talking together until an accord is reached. More precisely, Quakers are *listening* together, to each other and to the Spirit, for guidance. When a decision is reached, it is called *coming to unity.* There is unity as the community finds its way forward.

It isn't necessarily the most efficient method of decision making, but there are other benefits. Each person is committed to helping shape the final conclusion, and each insight is carefully assessed for the wisdom inherent in it, even when it contradicts other suggestions. If the discussion ends without coming to unity, the clerk who moderates the discussion sums up the situation by describing the *sense of the meeting,* noting what is clear and where there is agreement in the community and what is still unclear and undecided.

What wisdom does this tradition hold for individual discernment? As Thomas Kelly points out above, each of us holds within us "a whole committee of selves." With a clamor of inner selves pulling in different directions, we are like a community trying to make a decision. Even if you haven't *come to unity* yet, this chapter suggests that we find the *sense of the meeting* for our inner selves. This is a time to review and reflect on what is clear and what is not, and, in so doing, bring further clarity to our decision making.

THE COMPLEXITY OF DISCERNMENT

Thus far we have focused on the first two strands of decision making, a willing spirit and an attentive mind and heart. In this section, we turn to the third strand—*responsiveness*—which has been present all along, braided into your work on those first two strands. As you have cultivated your willingness and your attentiveness, you have been responding as well. You are responding when you open to the Spirit and attend to its wisdom, when you respect your fears and learn from them. You are responding as you have been engaged in the practices to learn about yourself and your situation. Your way forward may be clearer now. Perhaps you've made a decision and are beginning to live it out, finding new choices to be made along the way.

What you may also have discovered is a deeper awareness of the complexity of the decision before you. Our desires may be contradictory, as my friend Nora found when she recently broke her leg. While she was laid up with her leg in a cast, she discovered for the first time how much she loved having spaciousness in her life, how much she valued the quieter pace that her incapacity forced on her. When she recovered, she said, she wanted to keep up her volunteer work, her part-time job, and her friendships, but she also wanted to create more space and a slower pace for her daily life. "Can I," she wondered, "keep the feeling of spaciousness I've grown to love without giving up anything?" In the midst of her seemingly contradictory desires, Nora knew she had a freshly formed habit of slowed and spacious living that she wanted to incorporate as she recovered mobility. As a result, her discernment focused on the attitudes and activities that would nurture that way of living. She decided to begin with one day a week in which she would not have any appointments, a Sabbath day that would be marked on her calendar.

Nora only needed to consider her own desire and schedule when she made her decision, but many decisions are made in collaboration with others. When a couple's deeply held opinions and longings are involved, the factors to consider are exponentially increased. With more people comes more complexity—what is best for the children, for the aging parents, for the business partners?

Last autumn my daughter Diana wanted to cut a few half-days from her full-time job to have more time with her small children. First she needed to persuade her business associates that it was a good idea. Could she do her share of the work in fewer hours? Then she and her husband needed to piece together a child-care network out of disparate puzzle pieces that weren't going to add up to a whole. There was day care, preschool, grandparent care, Mom's mornings at home, and Dad's emergency availability. Which day care and preschool were available, not too distant, and had a loving atmosphere? Which would take one child, which two, how much did they cost, and how long were they open each day? Many families are familiar with this kind of complex decision making, where there is no right answer, but they forge the best decision they can out of what is at hand. Imperfect is often as good as it gets.

When all aspects of the decision incline us in one direction, the decision is easily made. The decision unfolds naturally; we may not even be consciously aware that we are making it. For example, I didn't *decide* to create a garden any more than I decided not to go skydiving when my husband chose to try it. Neither of those "decisions" made me stop and think about them. The difficult decisions are those between equally good paths, all with subpaths branching from them. We must choose, yet none of the options is absolutely and clearly right. Perhaps there is temporal pressure: We must decide *now* but we don't know enough to decide. What happens then? Should we just close our eyes and jump?

So, although you may be clear about your path at this point, it is equally possible that you feel as if you're lost in a fog. It may seem more like bushwhacking through a jungle than a clearly defined path that is going somewhere. Sometimes it is tempting to turn away or run away from the need to decide. We might conclude that it's all too hard and we don't want to think about it anymore. I encourage you to keep on, because it is precisely at those dark places that divine Light can illuminate the darkness.

Rose Mary Dougherty of the Shalem Institute for Spiritual Formation reminded my class of spiritual directors that when we feel pulled forward, backward, and sideways all at once, we need to take off our shoes. Like Moses, we're on holy ground. It is usually at those times when we hear so many contradictory voices speaking within and around us that we most need to stop and open to the Spirit. We remain confused, but there can grow within us just enough trust to believe that the way will be illuminated before us.

It is valuable to remember that discerning the way is a sacred process, even when we have to move ahead without a clear sense of how it will turn out, even when we move ahead into a fog and feel it whirling around us. The philosopher Friedrich Nietzsche wrote, "I tell you: one must have chaos within oneself to give birth to a dancing star." The path through uncertainty is often the path we follow. Paying attention as best we can and then, with God's help, stepping out into the unknown, can birth the brightest dancing star we can create in an imperfect world.

As you review what you've discovered through your efforts to make a decision, be prepared to find more clarity. The practices at the end of this chapter will open you to more insights, even though they review what you have already explored. The clarity of your decision may surprise you when it comes.

TESTING OUR DECISIONS

How do we test the conclusions we reach in decision making? Sometimes we test a decision by taking one step to try it out, like checking the water temperature by dipping in one toe before jumping in. At other times we test a decision by waiting—will I feel differently by tomorrow or next week? Chapters 8 and 9 focus on these ways of testing our decisions. In this section we will look at the kinds of considerations that are raised by the cultural norms and assumptions by which we live.

Our decision making is so heavily influenced by factors ingrained in our consciousness that we don't even notice them. We are like people working in a chocolate factory who no longer notice the smell of chocolate. In a similar way, our decision making faculties have accommodated themselves to unexamined cultural standards, and often we don't notice the assumptions we have grown up with and have become accustomed to. Because we hardly know they are there, these norms may lead us to make decisions without considering whether their guidance in this specific situation is appropriate and wise at this time. For example, in our culture, career advancement is considered a good thing. Friends shower us with congratulations even before we consider what accepting a promotion will mean in our lives, even before we consider how the greater responsibility, additional hours at work, or increased salary will impact our days.

Since cultural expectations influence our decisions so much, we need to know what they are. We need to be able to see them clearly so that we are free of their unconscious influence. We may find we still agree with many of our cultural "givens" and note their wisdom, while others may carry less weight, but still deserve our consideration. And some of them we may decide to set aside at this time, for this decision.

Choosing to discard cultural norms even temporarily may feel scary. It is good to remember that the great spiritual leaders of the world have regularly clashed with the standards of their cultures. Two thousand years ago, Jesus dined regularly with outcasts, preached about giving away all our belongings, and had harsh words for those who valued strict observance of the law above compassion for the individual. Twenty-five hundred years ago on the other side of the world, a young man named Siddhartha, raised in a palace as a prince, was expected to become a great warrior and statesman. Instead, he turned away from the conventional life of a young man in his social station to embrace a life of poverty and to seek meaning and enlightenment, finding a deep, interconnected bond with all beings. As the Buddha, he taught the way of compassion and reverence for life, the important first precept of Buddhism then and now.

Important cultural assumptions of our own day include those listed below. You may have others to add to the list.

Is this safe? Will this build security for me and mine? What kind of safety and security is important to us and how much is enough? There may be situations where careful discernment leads us to conclude that even though the decision carries risk, it is clearly the direction in which we need to go. My friend Joe, for example, who leads peacemaking workshops in Israel and Palestine, describes his work as "safe enough." He is careful and sensitive to his surroundings, while still following the clear call of the work. If safety is the most important standard for decision making, we live in fear; if safety is dismissed entirely, we may have forgotten that our lives are interwoven with those of others and that they will suffer if we suffer. Where is the balance at this time, in this decision?

Is it likely to be successful? How are we defining success? We don't usually quarrel with success. In our culture, success stands as the premier standard for measuring the outcome of a decision. But what is often missing in the discussion is what defines success. Winning the championship constitutes a success, but so does reaching the finals. If, as Mother Teresa says, we are called to faithfulness rather than success, does faithfulness itself constitute success? Suppose a service agency that provides free food and clothing to the needy loses its funding and the board of advisors makes the painful decision to close the project. They need to remember the years of faithful service they gave to the community and resist the conclusion that they failed. Or perhaps we choose to take a stand in an uphill battle against an injustice because we cannot remain silent; success lies in simply taking the stand. The experience of having a carefully made decision blocked by a closed door can teach us something valuable, so success may lie in achieving that new wisdom. Success as a standard in decision making is only valuable when we carefully define what it means each time.

Does it lead to independence? Western culture values independence of mind and thought, and it respects individuals who make it on their own. We associate being independent with being strong, which is why we sometimes resist accepting assistance or advice. It is useful to consider in which areas of our lives independence is vital and in which we are willing to ask for help. Is the need to be independent ever a false guide? Is a need to be autonomous steering us away from a wise decision? For example, people often want to take on a physically challenging adventure on their own, like backpacking alone in the wilderness. But if there is no cell-phone access and no contact arrangement has been put in place, this decision to be independent is definitely unwise. Does a need to be autonomous ever steer you toward an unwise decision?

Will I gain in status or prestige? A cousin to success, status is ingrained in the decision making of our culture. Climbing the career ladder is admired; being satisfied with the status quo is merely acceptable. Qualifications and credentials open many career doors, but sometimes we want that degree or credential for the status it brings as well. I remember how gratifying I found the respect that came to me with my psychologist's license! How important is prestige in your decision making, and how much weight would you like it to carry?

Will it bring happiness? This is a tricky question because happiness comes in such a variety of forms. If I decide to go on a cruise because of the pictures of graceful young couples on boats having a wonderful time, and I forget that I need large chunks of solitude to be happy, a cruise might be a miserable vacation for me. Cultural standards of happiness focus on people enjoying themselves, receiving love, and having beautiful things, leading us to conclude that if we only had what others have, we'd be happy, too. Happiness may be better understood as a byproduct of the decisions we make that are deeply and authentically right for us. The cultural image of happiness as a standard in decision making is fallible and frequently false.

ALTERNATIVE STANDARDS FOR DECISION MAKING

Being aware of the cultural assumptions that play a role in our decisions is important, but it is also essential to look at other standards that are not as closely linked to our culture. The following guidelines remind us of our desire to have our choices be in harmony with God's ways.

Is this decision sacred? Is it holy? Oftentimes, everyday decisions are not thought of as sacred or holy. We may understand some major life choices as sacred and even sacramental (like marriage), but often such choices are simply seen as the "big ones" (like buying a house). However, if we decide to create our lives with God as our partner, all decisions become sacred decisions. Opening ourselves and our circumstances to God is a holy act, making everything from investments to vacation plans sacred. When Anne decided to take a bus trip to Williamsburg with her mother, she did it only because her mother needed a companion. She felt obliged to accompany her, but not eager to take the trip. But when she started thinking of the trip as a sacred choice to spend time with her mother, it completely changed her experience. What difference does it make when you think of the decision you are making as a sacred and holy act?

Is this mine to do? Sometimes we see an area of need, a task that is waiting to be carried out, and we feel we must do something about it. How can we choose *not* to do it? In *A Testament of Devotion,* Thomas Kelly reminds us that "the Loving Presence does not burden us equally with all things, but considerately puts upon each of us just a few central tasks, as emphatic responsibilities. For each of us, these special undertakings are our share in the joyous burden of love." What wise words! There are so many needs to respond to. Which need is yours? Is the work, volunteer effort, service project, or cause that is tugging at you really yours to do? And what part of this work is yours to do?

Will this decision do the least harm? The effects of our decisions ripple outward, and we can't see clearly all the shores they will touch. Nevertheless, this is an important question. When none of the paths before us is completely right, considering which is likely to be the least harmful can help. Jill and Jonah knew that remodeling their house would affect the environment, so they tried to choose materials that would do the least harm. They used sustainably harvested hardwood flooring and nontoxic paints, and they were delighted to find a beautiful old door at a store selling recycled building materials.

Is this decision congruent with others we have made wisely? Past decisions can help us realize when we have made a wise decision. Is this decision part of a recognizable pattern of decisions, part of a pattern of God's nudges in our lives? A decision that differs from this pattern is not necessarily wrong, but it is wise to consider how and why it differs. Perhaps a turning point has been reached and a different path lies ahead. The new path (retirement decisions, for example) might be stirring up unease simply because it is new, not because it is unwise.

Is this Love's way? Though I use many names for God, the most important of these is Love. Is a decision loving? Does it arise from a place of love within us? A decision arising from love isn't necessarily easy or soft; it may appear strict or even harsh. A parental decision to cease supporting an adult child with an addiction is one example of love. So is a decision to open your home to a foster child. The test of love is a test of the heart, which only the person making the decision can answer: Does this decision spring from a loving heart?

CONSULTING THE COMMUNITY

Being part of a community in which we are known and cared for, a community where we feel we belong, is an invaluable aid to discernment. Such a community might be, for example, a religious group or parents group, or a book club made of up longtime friends. Community can be found at work or at the gym or in a Twelve Step program. In decision making, community support can make the difference between clarity and going around and around in the fog. If the community is a large one, we need a smaller circle within it, a few wise and trusted people we are especially close to. They can help us review our decision and sort out the options. With them it's possible to share what we've learned, and look at the pieces of our complex decisions. We trust them to hear us and provide a safe place for speaking out, a safe place from which to step forth.

In Quaker communities there is a small listening group called the *clearness committee*. It is a precious tool for decision making, for discerning the way with the help of a few wise and trusted friends. The basic assumption underlying the work of the clearness committee is that we each have an Inner Guide or

Teacher with more wisdom than we can access alone. The group helps the person facing a decision to listen to that wisdom more deeply. Members of the group listen, pay attention without judging, and help to clarify alternatives. They encourage the person to find the truth she needs. They do not provide answers, but instead give space for the answers to surface through spacious silent reflection and thoughtful questioning. Even when a clear decision is not reached, the process always brings movement and some new insights for the ongoing process of making decisions. Bringing tangled, contradictory motives and confusion to a clearness committee, a person receives patience and understanding as everyone helps to untangle the knots and find clear strands of insight.

What is the gift of listening? When we are truly listened to, we hear our own words better. We say out loud what may have only been whispered within our minds or possibly written in a journal. Good listeners provide space—space for the spoken words to sink in and for new understanding to arise. In ordinary conversation, we lob the conversational ball back and forth, each of us taking a turn to talk about ourselves. In this listening conversation, we remain focused on the specific discernment questions that are being raised.

Occasionally, listeners who know and love us begin to adopt our decision as their own. They make suggestions; they fill our ears with advice. For example, they would take the risk of opening a small business, so they urge us to do it. Or they tell us the decisions they made about caring for infirm parents and they seem to think our situation is comparable. We may gain valuable insight and understanding from them, but sometimes the advice-giver hasn't grasped the uniqueness of our particular situation and his advice is not helpful.

We would all like to have a community of support, people who can listen nonjudgmentally as we work our way through challenging decisions. Perhaps you are reflecting on how your circles fall short. Perhaps you are recognizing with gratitude a community to which you belong. Remember that both organized and informally gathered groups can provide a trusted circle of support.

Before concluding that there is no one who will listen and support you, try this: From all those who cross your path, which two or three people would you choose as supportive and trust-worthy listeners, even if you don't know them well? Can you risk asking them whether they would help you as you sort out a deci-sion? You could talk one-on-one or gather a small group to meet with you. It may be a gift for your listener to be asked, as well as a gift for you to open yourself up and take that step. Every time I have asked a couple of friends to meet with me, I have hesitated because I know how busy they are. But they have been honored to be asked, pleased to be so trusted and respected that I would turn to them.

If there is no one you feel you can turn to within your com-munity, but you still think that talking it out could help, turn to a professional—a trained listener, such as a counselor, a coach, a spiritual director, or the leader of your religious community. A professional listener provides the wisdom of experience and the detachment that friends sometimes can't give. As a psychologist and as a spiritual director, I have often heard people say that my listening to them was the most helpful part of our session together. Once a counselor told me that he wanted to listen to a client until "she could hear her own heart's knowing."

I have emphasized the value of small groups and supportive friendships as aids in decision making, but simply belonging to a spiritual community itself can bring us hope and help us find our way. We are not alone; we are surrounded by others who worship the Spirit and honor its wisdom. Being with such others on a reg-ular basis helps us remember to turn to the Spirit's wisdom for our own individual path. Sitting in worship with a community strengthens us to continue the journey of discernment.

Practices for Finding Your Way

These practices help you review all the different facets of your decision. Take your time with them as you evaluate where you are in the decision-making process and remain open to new insights.

LOOKING AT THE THEMES

This practice examines the characteristic themes of your discernment process, those aspects of your decision that keep weaving their way through your thoughts and feelings. Taking notes is important here. This practice is a good one to use with a friend or two or with a spiritual director who is accompanying you on this journey of discernment. Explain that you need them to listen as you review your situation, and then you want to discuss it with them.

1. Bring together any notes you have gathered in your discernment process, any information on options or understandings about yourself that are important for this decision. Review journal entries and your responses to earlier practices in this book.
2. Review what you have done, thought, observed, or felt as part of this process. Even when you don't have written notes, recall what you experienced as you explored aspects of yourself and your situation.
3. What ideas, insights, feelings, or values arise repeatedly? This could include areas such as freedom, family, time, fear, compassion, or money. Why do they appear repeatedly?
4. Name two or three themes or values that seem to be most important and powerful to you. How are they reflected in the possibilities you are considering? What importance do you want them to have?

5. You may find that your review has helped you find new questions to consider—questions that need answers as part of coming to a decision. Spend some time with those questions.

THE BASELINE

This practice invites consideration of what absolute necessities an acceptable decision would need to have. I am not suggesting that you settle for the minimum, but it is helpful to know what it is.

1. Reflect on your situation with all its factors and consider what basics a right path needs to incorporate, including living necessities. For example, with all extras omitted, how much do you need to earn? What child care do you need? Is travel and other recreation a basic need of your life? Take time to consider the "bottom line" needs that this decision must allow for.
2. Do all of the possible outcomes of your decision meet the basic needs you've listed? What does it mean if they don't?

TRAVEL EACH PATH

In this practice, adapted from the Ignatian spiritual tradition, you use your imagination in your discernment. It is helpful to do this once you have narrowed your possible options to just a few, and you wish to examine them in greater depth. Set aside a half-hour or more to explore each possibility.

1. Find a quiet time when you will not be interrupted. Take the first possibility and imagine yourself living with that decision in your life as completely as you can. Imagine all the ways it shapes your life, becoming aware of feelings, physical states, physi-

cal settings, and your attitudes and thoughts as you live with that decision. Write down what you noticed as you were imagining, what you liked and what you didn't, what surprised you and what didn't—all the details that you imagined experiencing. Then set that aside for at least twenty-four hours.

2. On another day, take out the second possibility and repeat the process. Imagine as thoroughly as you can all the aspects of living out the decision. Write it all out and set it aside for a day or longer.

3. After repeating the practice with all the possibilities, review all your experiences. What do you notice about what you wrote down? What have you learned? What has been reaffirmed? Return at least one more time to review the experiences and gather more insights.

Standards for Decisions

This practice uses the ten standards from this chapter (see pages 120–124) to reflect on the choices you have made or are making and helps you look at your decision making standards over time.

1. Consider which of the ten standards for decision making are most important to you in this decision. Choose a few that stand out and write them down. You might also add something that is pivotal to you about this decision but was not included in this chapter.

2. Looking again at the standards, choose two or three that do not apply to this decision, and list them.

3. Recall who you were and what was important to you at another stage of your life. Remember where you lived, what you did, and how you lived. Would

your response to this exercise have been different then?

4. Take some time to reflect on what you have learned about the standards that you live by, recognizing that they describe you and what your values are.

STEP BY STEP

Live up to the Light thou hast, and more will be given to thee.

—*Caroline Fox,* Memories of Old Friends

"How are you doing these days?" she asked. It was just a casual question, but looking at her, I knew she really wanted an answer. The truth was that I was facing some major life decisions and wasn't doing all that well. But it was a conversation on Sunday after church, so I responded with a hearty "Just fine!"

Fortunately for me, Beverly was a wise woman who saw right through my words. She pulled me aside and insisted on the real story, listening intently as I stumbled through it. Finally, she spoke.

"Nancy," she said, "you are standing in darkness and you can't see the way forward. But you have a lantern in your hand that gives enough light to take one step. When you take that step, your lantern moves with you. It illuminates one more step. You will always have the lantern and there will always be one more step. What is your next step?"

Her words of wisdom have remained with me ever since. Whenever we take a step, we change things; we change the landscape of our decision making. As we stand in this new place, there is new light.

The next step can vary enormously. Sometimes the step is to seek further information. Suppose I've made a decision to work on improving my health. I may need a physical exam to find out more about my physical status. What is my cholesterol, my blood pressure? Perhaps I have to find out which gyms offer the kind of workout I'm looking for. Perhaps I need to read up on healthy eating, so I have to go to the bookstore or the library.

The decision may involve just a trial step or it may be a real leap, a "signing on the dotted line" commitment. Lynn just turned fifty and has tentatively decided to go back to school to study art in hopes of teaching someday. She takes it one course at a time. Each semester brings a fresh opportunity for discernment: Is this right for me? Is this an authentic next step? Why am I doing this? She is still testing the path; each step is a trial decision. Lynn's daughter is in graduate school, too. Unlike her mother, she committed herself to the complete program. She is not sure where her professional path is leading her, but she knows that she is traveling in the right direction by studying for a counseling degree.

ON THE THRESHOLD

There is a time for experimental steps and a time for steps of commitment. When I received the contract for this book, it lay on my kitchen counter for a week while I tiptoed around it. For months I had held my lantern high, taking one step after another—I'd created a framework for the book, sketched out potential chapters, and written an introduction. Was this path going anywhere? Did I really want it to go anywhere? Now it was time for a firm commitment, but I held back, hesitant, not knowing what the future would hold. Then I stepped over the threshold and signed the contract.

Most of us have hesitated on the threshold of a decision at one time or another, not sure about entering the new room that lies before us. We are almost certain what we have decided, but we still hold back. Although this is the room we want to enter, it isn't well lit, and we can't see into the corners. It's an unfamiliar place.

It is easier to cross the threshold when we have done our homework. We have explored the possibilities, considered how we'd live with various outcomes, learned to know ourselves in all our peculiarities, and consulted with people we consider wise. And we have opened it all to a loving God. When we've done all that, it's time to take the next step.

As Lynn and her daughter are discovering, there are many ways of stepping forward: one course at a time or committing to the whole program at once. For Lynn, the decision about graduate school is a heavy one, and she is cautiously moving forward. People experience the weight of their decisions differently, but relationship or career decisions are always among the big ones.

For example, people often hesitate for years on the threshold of the room called "divorce." It is an unknown and frightening room. But even for this difficult room, there are many separate steps we take to enter it. And we can take them one at a time. From initially thinking about separation to deciding how to handle finances and child custody to beginning to think of ourselves as single people—each step brings its own decisions, and it is understandable to hesitate before each one. Any major change in our lives is worth hesitating over, but no decision should have us permanently camped on the threshold.

Sometimes a decision that is easy for one person looms large for another. When Chad signed up for an exercise class, for example, it was a huge step for him. Never having been inside a commercial gym, he felt uncomfortable and self-conscious for weeks. Each week he had to decide all over again, "Yes, I'm going to do this."

Stepping forward into a decision requires sustained effort, the kind Chad made as he renewed his decision every time he went back to the gym. His decision to join a gym and exercise regularly is a good example of the dedicated commitment it takes to change a pattern of life. It is so much harder to change our habits than it is to know what needs to be changed. Recognizing the *need* to stop smoking, to go to a Twelve Step program, to break the evening TV habit with a class or volunteer work is one thing, but deciding to take the step and *do* it is the real challenge. Are there decisions you need to make about changing your life patterns? Chad made his decision after his physician told him his blood sugar was elevated. He received a "wake-up call," but we can also come to those decisions when something within ourselves simply says, "Yes, now is the time."

Oftentimes the pattern that we want to change involves more than our individual self. For forty years, Betsy's family celebrated the holidays at the family farm, but eventually the tradition no longer fit the family. The children had moved away and had their own celebrations now. It was time to create a new tradition, but she hesitated to speak out. She knew that hurt feelings and misunderstandings within families could linger for years. Finally, she gathered her courage and offered several new possibilities for family gatherings, inviting her relatives to discuss what would suit them best. It took a long time, but they finally decided what was most important about their family gatherings and together reinvented a celebration that reflected that. The hardest part, she now remembers, was deciding to begin the conversation and risking being rejected or misunderstood.

Betsy stepped out boldly, but carefully. As we move into the decisions we have made, we need this careful boldness. We listen again to the Guide; we pay attention to what our lanterns show us on the path ahead. We test the ground as we stand on it, feeling its solidity, and then we take another step. We pay attention, we notice, and then we respond. With a unique blend of courage and caution, we weave together the strands of discernment into one continuous process.

LETTING GO OF OTHER OPTIONS
AND MOVING AHEAD

Someone once told me that taking the next step wasn't so hard, but it was very hard to let go of the unexplored possibilities of other paths. He wanted to hold on to all the possibilities. Letting go of the path not chosen can be hard, but walking forward while looking backwards regretfully is dangerous. That almost guarantees stumbling and falling. "Oh, the lives I could have lived!" is a sad lament.

If we've done the homework and the way opens clearly ahead, we can step forward gladly. But sometimes we have done the work and made the best decision possible, yet we're still not glad and eager. Was the decision forced? Perhaps we had to rush to meet an application deadline. Or we desperately needed a job, but the right kind of work wasn't offered. That's when the temptation to look backwards is strongest. That's when we need divine wisdom to help us live out the imperfect decision we've made.

Once a decision is made, the chosen path contains thousands of small daily decisions. Among the most important of them is the attitude we bring to our daily life, the disposition with which we walk the chosen path. "Walk cheerfully over the earth," says Quaker founder George Fox. What does it mean to "walk cheerfully"? Seeking out the small satisfactions of the moment, the small gifts of daily life, nurtures cheerfulness and gratitude. Pausing and paying attention, as described in chapter 6, helps maintain the attitude of walking cheerfully.

Fox continues by asking us to respond to "that of God in each person." Now there is an attitude-altering invitation! We are asked to see the sacred around us on this new path, which may feel far from sacred or perfect now that we are on it. We are asked to get to know the people on it and discover their hidden goodness. To fully live the decision we've made, we continually need to bring ourselves to this way of looking around us. After we make the decision, we still need divine Light to help us see our way and shape our daily living. We still need the divine Guide to help us "walk cheerfully" and to "see that of God in each person."

When Laura and Paul retired, they decided to move to rural upstate New York. Though they had lived and worked in suburban New Jersey, they had always looked forward to country life. However, it didn't turn out as they had hoped. Driving twenty miles to shop reminded them how easy it used to be to buy groceries. An old house and a large property took much more work than they had expected. The new friendships they had hoped for in the community weren't materializing, and occasional weekend guests from their old life didn't dispel their feeling of isolation.

Right now Laura and Paul are focusing on the losses involved in their decision. At some point, they may reconsider their decision and decide it was the wrong one for them. But they could also decide to stop looking backward, and begin the work of cultivating the gifts of their new life. They could respond to the adventure of growing into the new shape of their lives.

As we walk the carefully chosen path, we build its rightness for us. There is a wise saying that "the road is made by walking." We make the path not only by stepping over the threshold but through all the daily steps we take. Even more important, we make *ourselves* by how we walk the path. The attitude with which I walk the path shapes who I am and who I become.

THE REALITY OF SETBACKS

This section could also be called "The Reality of *Stepbacks*," since that is what really happens when we experience setbacks. A step forward is followed by one, two, even three steps back. Walking down the hall of opportunity, we discover that some doors are locked just as we were ready to go through them. What happens then?

My wise friend Beverly told me, "There is always a next step." It is easy to become discouraged and lose our momentum after the third step back, after the sixth door that doesn't open. I invite you to adopt this piece of wisdom as your mantra, repeating it as you keep on stepping out and trying those doors, as you look at another apartment to rent or as you check out more schools. Sometimes the next step is a matter of discovering which doors are firmly locked. Which companies are not hiring right now? Which preschools are filled? Which apartment complexes are too expensive?

Keep repeating, "There is always a next step" as you follow up on your decision to change a life pattern. Sometimes the setback comes from our own faltering resolution. Rise early to go running, even though you slept in all last week. Return to the yoga class, even though the moves still don't feel comfortable. Give the group you joined another chance. Keep coming back to your decision.

In dealing with setbacks, we need to closely weave together the three strands of discernment we have been considering throughout this book. We open ourselves to God's guidance, pay attention to all that we can notice, and then we respond with another step. For example, Laura and Paul, retired and living in upstate New York, might have adjusted to life in their rural community, but they eventually concluded that their decision to live in upstate New York was a mistake. While a rural life still appealed to them, *this* rural life did not. So what is their next step? It is time to return again to weaving the three strands of discernment. Opening themselves to God's guidance, they need to be carefully attentive to all they can observe about their present life that seems to fit them and all that doesn't. They need to explore every possibility open to them, considering finances, health, and friendships to discover the kind of life they want now.

Sometimes when it seems that a big decision is a mistake, we will find other methods of moving in the direction we've chosen. It may be time to take a big step back and survey the whole landscape. Are there other ways to incorporate something we truly want into our lives now? Are sideways steps possible? Be creative with what is possible.

Once I met with a woman who had been estranged from her brother for over ten years. As she grew older, she decided to reconnect with him and his family, and imagined having their holidays and summer picnics together. Unfortunately, he wasn't interested. After trying for a year to build a relationship, she stepped back and reconsidered. Finally, deciding all over again that she did want some relationship with her brother, she adjusted her idea of what it would be. She would send holiday cards, occasional chatty e-mails, and sometimes invitations for special occasions. This is not the relationship she wanted, but she is determined to cultivate the relationship she can have.

In facing setbacks, the most important quality you need is perseverance. There is a program in my town called Job Club for people who have lost their jobs. It is open to all, but participants must agree that, following a week of orientation and training, they will *keep on trying* to get a job until they succeed. Job Club provides the support and accountability of peers and free access to phones and computers, but all the club members need to do the hard work themselves.

Starting again, trying another approach, paying attention to a new lead, and continuing to come to Job Club—all that is hard work. But it is easier to persevere when we are not alone, when a whole group of us are in it together. Setbacks of any kind are easier to face with companionship. A group or perhaps just one friend who gives support and encouragement and to whom we are accountable strengthens us as we step forward yet again.

Sometimes the setback is more like a door closing. Chris was skilled at his work in fund-raising, but quite unsatisfied by it. He kept the job because he needed to earn a living for himself and his family. His passion was altogether different: He longed to create a traveling theater company that would teach and perform on issues of social justice. But with little extra money and even less time, he didn't know how to make it happen.

Then a door closed: Chris suddenly lost his job. The setback was an opportunity to reconsider the shape of his work life. Could he draw closer to the work he longed for and still earn a living? Was there paid work that would be more in line with his dream, perhaps a job where he would learn and earn? He doesn't know whether his dream will ever become a reality, but he does know that losing his job forced him to explore his desire for a different, more satisfying work life.

TRUSTING THE RIVER

Many years ago my husband, Larry, and I took a raft trip down the Grand Canyon with a group of friends. As we floated down the Colorado River the first glorious morning, basking in the hot sun and admiring the massive stone walls around us, Larry inquired of our guide, Duffy, "Where will we be having our picnic lunch?" And Duffy responded serenely, "The river will tell us." Later in the day, Larry raised another question: "Where do you expect to camp tonight?" And once again Duffy responded, "The river will tell us." My husband says he learned an important lesson on that trip. Floating down the river is floating into the unknown. Though the guide knew the river, he didn't know the river of this trip. He didn't know what picnic and camping spots would be filled with other rafts or what sand bars would still be there for our landing. He trusted the river, and remained open to its possibilities.

Any time we hold our lanterns high and step forward, we are embarking on the unknown, on a new adventure. No matter how well we've prepared, something unexpected will happen. We need to be attentive to the river we're on, observing what is happening along the way, and responding to the situations we encounter. Like Duffy, we have to steer the raft as best we can, but we also need to trust the river.

We have to trust that the answers we seek will come, that places to eat and rest will present themselves. We need to trust the organic process of taking step after step. Each step changes our perspective of the landscape; each step changes us. That is why the person who starts out to reach a goal is not the same person who reaches it. That person has been changed by the journey itself. Can we trust the change to which we're opening ourselves? Can we trust the unknown when we can't know what lies around the next bend? Two gifts for travelers can help us trust in what lies ahead of us.

TRAIL ANGELS

The longest hiking trail in the United States is the Pacific Crest Trail. Each summer dedicated hikers challenge themselves to hike its entire length. Last year my French friend Jean-Michel fulfilled a lifelong dream by hiking it. He prepared carefully, becoming an expert on the trail long before leaving France. He chose his equipment carefully, conditioned his body, and a friend agreed to send him supplies at post offices along the way.

But even though Jean-Michel prepared well, the most unexpected blessings he encountered were trail angels. Found along both the Appalachian and Pacific Crest trails, trail angels are people who drop off gifts at the sleeping huts: Hikers discover big barrels of fresh water or shopping bags filled with energy bars. Sometimes there is more. Trail angels invited Jean-Michel into their homes for meals and showers, and drove him to nearby towns to pick up mail and replace supplies.

Trail angels can be found on all our trails. Whether it is the fellow seekers at the Job Club or the unexpected phone call that comes when it is needed most, trail angels are everywhere. Sometimes it is hard for us to acknowledge our needs. We might reply, "Just fine," as I did when Beverly asked me how I was doing. It is even harder to reach out for help. When we do, however, we experience the miracle of a casual friend or a perfect stranger transforming himself into a trail angel.

THE SPIRIT AS ADVOCATE

Trail angels are one gift to the traveler who is stepping out into the unknown. The second gift is the availability of the Spirit as a continual presence. "Lead me to the rock that is higher than I," requests the psalmist in Psalm 61. We all need a rock to depend on that is higher than ourselves. We need a wisdom greater than our own and a strength greater than our own.

In the Gospel of John, Jesus promises an "Advocate" who will be with us as a companion. *Advocate* is a good word in this context. It is a person who is on your side, who sticks with you, speaks up for you, and generally looks out for your welfare. John described this advocate as "the Spirit of truth" (John 15:26). The Spirit, the Advocate, does not perfectly smooth out the path as we step into the unknown. Hard times happen. But the Spirit is biased in our favor and lovingly accompanies us as we venture into the unknown.

~~⌒

This book is grounded in the image of weaving a braid whose three sections fit snugly together and create a long, strong strand. Each section of the braid—*willingness, attentiveness,* and *responsiveness*—is woven in turn into the center. Each strand is dependent on the others for its strength. Here, in the *responsiveness* section, we see how they turn and turn again to each other for strength. Paying attention leads to responding with a step. We step forth trusting and open to the Light to illuminate and show the way forward. And so it continues: Pay attention, trust, step forth.

Practices for Finding Your Way

These are practices to use while you step into a new facet of your life. However, you also need to pay attention to how things change for you as you take steps forward, to notice the new landscape of your path as you move ahead. You may find it helpful to revisit attentiveness practices earlier in the book.

Two Steps a Week
The only step you need to take is the next one. This practice asks you to commit to two steps a week and to take those steps. It is important to write out this practice.

1. You have made a decision and are ready to move forward. Perhaps your decision is only provisional and uncertain, but you are going to act on it. Write down two things you will do to implement your decision this week. Whether small or large, you are willing to take these steps.
2. Under each step you plan to take, list the strengths and skills that will help you take that step. Acknowledge to yourself that you have these strengths and skills and that you will use them as you move forward.
3. Then list any obstacles that could interfere with your forward progress—perhaps blocks within yourself or external stumbling blocks. For each potential barrier, write out at least one way you can manage or overcome it so it will not hold you back.
4. Write down when you will take each step (or begin taking it).
5. After you have met your commitment for this week, take notes about what was helpful in this practice. Then prepare for the next week and the next steps you will commit to.

The Accountability Friend
We all need support and encouragement from others. This practice describes one way of arranging for that accountability and support.

1. Carefully think about who could be an "accountability friend" for you, someone you trust to support you and with whom you can be honest and open. The friend needs to be willing to ask you about the steps you have committed to take and must not be afraid to ask you how you plan to get moving again if you are stuck.

2. Before you ask someone to be an accountability friend, make sure you understand specifically what you are asking for. What kind of regular contact do you need? Perhaps you want a weekly e-mail exchange or perhaps you want to meet face-to-face. How long is this accountability relationship going to last? Are you asking for a commitment of six weeks or six months? You and your accountability friend will decide on the details together, but it is important to consider in advance the arrangement you'd like to have.

3. Having asked someone to be an accountability friend, you may discover that your friend would like to receive the same gift from you. An equal exchange can deepen your friendship. On the other hand, do not be discouraged if someone turns you down. Your friend may be uncomfortable with this role, but still be loving and supportive. Ask someone else.

4. As you begin, talk to your friend about the background of your decision. Be specific about your decision and what your next step is going to be.

5. Tell your friend when you have taken the next step. Share any problems you found along the way and what you plan to do next.

Opening to the Spirit

When you open the decision you've made and the steps you are taking to the Spirit, you are offering your individual situation to the larger tapestry of God's sacred weaving.

1. Find a time and place where you can be quiet, comfortable, and uninterrupted. Give yourself a few minutes to settle into it. Notice your breathing as you relax into an awareness of the present moment. Acknowledge that the Spirit is present, even if you aren't feeling anything special at the moment.

2. Consciously offer your decision to the Spirit. Opening your hands or arms may help you. Find words to express your openness, such as "Loving God, this is the decision I have made, the path I am walking."

3. Acknowledge that your path is a work in progress, and ask for more wisdom to guide your further steps. Consider what the next steps may be, and open them to the Spirit.

4. Close with a time for gratitude and gladness for the presence of the Spirit.

A MANTRA FOR SPIRITUAL RENEWAL

As you move forward into your decisions, be sure to continue daily practices of spiritual awareness. In a time of change, you can lose your balance by either tilting too quickly into the future or encountering setbacks. In addition to those offered earlier in the book, the following suggestions may be helpful.

1. Find a mantra or repetitive prayer that you can return to repeatedly throughout the day. The purpose of the word or sentence is to remember, during other activities, what is of central importance to you, what is at your core.

2. Carry a small object that has sacred meaning to you—a stone or a circle of beads, a small shell, or

any other sacred symbol—and touch it often. It could be in your pocket, your car, or your desk. Like a mantra, its purpose is to bring you once again to remember who you truly are, to remember that you want to live a life guided by God.

CHAPTER NINE

WHEN WE HAVE TO WAIT

*You're allowing your soul to grow up. If you can't be
still and wait, you can't become what God created you
to be.*

—*Sue Monk Kidd,* When the Heart Waits

I write this on a cold, windy February day. It has been a day of
waiting. During these last few days, southern Pennsylvania
received a record-breaking forty inches of snow, and now all of
it is blowing across the fields in front of my home, sculpted by
blizzard winds into spectacular drifts. We're securely snowed in.
I've canceled plans, put off errands, and puttered around the
house.

Today, however, I am not only waiting for the snowplow
(although it will probably take a front-end loader to clear out the
driveway), but I'm also waiting for a death. My cat Strider is
dying. We've done all we can for him, and now he simply lies by
me as I stroke his head and talk to him and watch his chest rise
and fall. He's still breathing and I'm still waiting.

Waiting is not a popular pursuit in our culture. We live in an
age of activity, achievement, and arrival—the sooner the better.
We're surrounded by fast lanes, high-speed Internet, and instant
everything; waiting is wasted time. We don't like to wait and I

think the underlying reason we don't like it is that it makes us feel helpless. While waiting, we become aware of our human limitations. I cannot do anything about the storm or Strider's slowly approaching death. I cannot make something happen. All I can do is be with what is happening. The activity of waiting is *being with.*

It may seem strange to look at waiting times as part of *responsiveness,* but waiting goes hand in hand with taking steps. Like sleep and wakefulness, times of waiting and times of moving forward are both essential parts of daily life. They are both essential to decision making. Waiting is actually not empty and profitless, but a full and necessary stage of living. What happens while we wait is often something that can happen no other way.

In the *Tao Te Ching*, the ancient classic of Chinese Taoism, the questions are raised: "Do you have the patience to wait until your mud settles and the water is clear? Can you remain unmoving until the right action arises by itself?" Clear water, clear knowing, and the right time for the next step come as we are patient and wait.

WHY WE WAIT

Robin has owned and operated a school for children with learning disabilities for many years. Though he loves teaching and he loves the children, he has become very tired and is ready to lay down the never-ending responsibility of running the school. He wants to sell the property, close the school, and embark on the next stage of his life. He has done his discernment homework. He's paid attention to his finances, his life situation, and his gifts, and he is ready to move on. He's eager to travel, and is thinking about spending the next few years traveling around the world, spending a month here or there as he wishes. But he needs to sell the property first, and right now no one wants to buy it, no matter how desirable he tries to make it. Robin is clear about his next step, but he can't take it yet.

Unlike Robin, Carla could embark upon her next step right now, but she has chosen to wait because the time is not yet ripe. She dreams of being a nurse in the mountains of Tennessee. She grew up there and she's eager for the challenge of working in a totally different setting from the suburban hospital where she works now. But she has two adolescents at home whom she does not want to uproot at this time. She has accepted the need to wait for a few years until the time is right.

Like Carla, we may sometimes choose to postpone a dream or, like Robin, be forced into a time of waiting. But at other times we may wait because we ourselves don't understand enough about the path or which choice is best. Despite faithfully paying attention and trying to notice God's nudges, clarity and certainty elude us. Even after discerning the direction in which to move, we can be paralyzed by the question of timing. Is this the right time to take this step? Should I wait longer?

My husband is a devoted nature photographer. In our forty years together, I have learned that nature photographers think nothing of waiting hours for the perfect light. Once, as he explained yet again his need to wait for the sun to come out, a friend commented, "You know, you can wait half your life for the sun to come out."

Our friend wasn't talking about photography, but about a habit of living. We *can* wait too long for the sun to come out; we can wait so long that waiting becomes procrastination, an avoidance of hard truths or uncomfortable steps. We keep hoping the other person will change, or the situation we're stuck in will improve. How long is too long to wait? And how do we know it?

One of the challenges of spiritual discernment is that wise advice is frequently contradictory. There's a traditional Quaker saying: *Don't run ahead of the Guide.* I agree with that, but I also think that we *make the path by walking it.* Which advice should we heed?

The answer, I think, lies within. If we have been carefully attentive to our life circumstances, our gifts and skills, and the passion of our hearts, and we are still not clear about waiting or stepping forth, we need to look inside ourselves again. What motivates our waiting or our stepping forth? When we are highly attentive to our varied impulses, we begin to discern those that arise out of fear or out of our ego's needs, as opposed to those that seem firmly grounded in divine wisdom. For example, if I notice that a big motivation for writing a book is to be admired by my friends or to feel more important, that means my ego is guiding my decision. I need to hear again, *Don't run ahead of the Guide.* Perhaps I don't need to stop, but I do need to be more attentive to the Spirit's nudges. Perhaps I need to walk, instead of run. But if I notice that I avoid writing a book out of fear, I need to hear again, *Make the path by walking it.* Since our motivations are usually a colorful tangle of desires, biases, insecurities, and hunger for God, we need as much light as possible. Opening ourselves, our motivations, and the whole complex situation to the divine Light helps us understand whether it is time for waiting or whether we are avoiding the journey we need to take.

WHAT'S HAPPENING IN THE WAITING

Ever since I was a child, I've loved Christmas. I love the holiday with all its attendant traditions—hearing the music, decorating the tree and the house, gathering with family and friends, exchanging gifts, and attending the Christmas Eve candlelight service. And I must admit the first Christmas carols are heard at my house sometime in November, because for me Christmas is not a day on the calendar but a season, and a way of living in that season. Sometimes friends who don't understand this will ask me in mid-December if I am "ready for Christmas." They don't understand that I am already in it. It has already begun.

There are two ways to experience waiting. The first is to wait *for* something. Perhaps we are waiting, like Robin and

Carla, for the building to sell or the teenagers to grow up. Or perhaps we're waiting for the phone to ring or for December 25 to come. But the second way is to wait *while* something is happening. Look around: Perhaps Christmas is already happening. Perhaps what is happening while we wait is something essential to the unfolding of the decision—only we can't see it yet.

When we wait *for* something, we are just marking time until the "real" living begins. By focusing on the future, we are not fully living the present, not fully aware of the events and people filling the waiting time. What is happening *while* we wait? This time is shaping us, though we may not be aware of it. Even if we didn't choose to wait, we can decide how to live through it. The invitation of a waiting time is to be alive in it, to notice how we are being shaped and what is being called forth while we wait. Waiting has its own unique gifts. We can resist the gifts or try to receive them with grace. What are the gifts of waiting?

A devoted bird-watcher told me that many people think they need to keep on walking in order to find birds. But "The best way," she said, "is to walk for a while and then stop and wait; sit down on a fallen log." Something will happen. "Maybe it won't be a new bird sighting," she added, "but I may notice a tiny yellow wildflower tucked under a dead leaf or the way the sunlight plays in puddles across the forest floor." She is awake to what is happening while she waits, and sees the miracles before her. She is receiving the gifts of waiting.

The Hebrew Scriptures teach that fields are to lie fallow every seventh year as a Sabbath for the land (Leviticus 25:1–12). During this time, the land is to be neither cultivated nor watered, but simply renewed through rest. The renewal of the fields, and of the vines and trees that cover them, is subtle and not readily apparent. On the surface, things may seem unchanged; what is happening is going on deep underneath. Renewal through our time of waiting, our time of lying fallow, is equally subtle. If we can accept it as a time of rest, it helps us understand what is going on. It is an opportunity to rest from the effort of reaching a decision, of preparing for a change. Waiting brings us rest and renewal and energizes us for the future.

Sometimes we are fortunate enough to know we're not ready for the next step even if the way is open. When Sue turned down a request to be president of the local church council, it wasn't because she had no time or interest in the work, but because she wasn't ready. It wasn't her time yet. Someday she might be ready with the confidence and skills to lead the council, but she wisely realized these gifts would only come with time, so she was willing to wait. Such knowing can be hard to explain to others, and hard to explain to ourselves as well, but it is true wisdom to recognize that the time is not right. In the words with which we began this chapter, our souls need time to grow up. While we wait, we are growing into who we need to be so that we can move forward.

A waiting time can be a time of transformation, akin to the caterpillar in its chrysalis. What was a caterpillar is wholly transformed into a butterfly during this time of outer stillness and inner transformation, this time of mystery and miracle. As much as we'd like to be butterflies, we would rather avoid the intermediate stage if we could. However, the caterpillar doesn't become a monarch butterfly while it is crawling around munching milkweed; it needs the time in the chrysalis for its glorious transformation. It needs to wait.

Of course, the caterpillar doesn't know that its chrysalis is a place of transformation, nor that it will become a butterfly. Neither do we understand the transformation that can happen in and through our waiting. But while we are biding our time, seemingly passive, something is happening. If we can trust in that, we can bear the time with better grace and with more patience.

As human beings in relationship with the Divine, we can participate in what happens while we wait. We bring our willingness and are open to the opportunities within the waiting. We bring our attentiveness—perhaps reviewing the decision we've made to reaffirm it or to discover an interim step we are ready to take.

Most importantly, by acknowledging a desire to grow spiritually during this time of waiting, we shape a way of waiting that will help us grow. We might want to grow more patient, or perhaps we'll focus on channeling our energy toward compassionate understanding. Living through times of waiting requires a daily renewal of our intention. It isn't easy to grow spiritually at such times; it is easier to fret. But waiting *will* change us, and we can choose to welcome the waiting with the intention of growing spiritually during this waiting time.

What spiritual growth do you want to nurture while you are waiting? Naming our intention strengthens the desire. A brief repeated prayer or mantra, like "I choose love," can renew in us our desire to be open to growing during this time. It helps us remember that we are not just waiting *for* something to happen, but *while* something is already happening. Although it may be hidden even from our view, within the chrysalis, the butterfly is forming and gathering strength.

During waiting times, it is very helpful to have a friend, a listening companion who will help us sort it all out and patiently wait with us. A friend who waits with us reminds us that something is happening even when it seems as if nothing is happening. Such a friend may see the gifts of the waiting more clearly than we can. Take a moment to consider who in your life could walk with you through a waiting time.

WAITING IN DARKNESS

It is hard to speak hopefully of the gifts of waiting when your heart is heavy and you feel helpless and discouraged. Waiting can be very painful. We may feel as if we are bulbs in winter hidden deep below the cold ground; we know we have *something* within us, but it's hard to believe that the cold and darkness form a necessary stage for future flourishing, or that the opportunity for blooming will ever come. But spring bulbs like tulips and daffodils do need a time of winter cold and darkness to bloom. Their growth is triggered when the earth warms after several months of cold and darkness. Meanwhile, they wait, snug and secure, trusting that spring will come. In our human waiting in darkness, we aren't usually secure or trusting. What helps us through our dark waiting times?

We can gear ourselves up to face something if we know it will end, and when it will end. Indefinite waiting is much harder. When Andrea lost her job, she was sure she'd find another one quickly, but months passed, and she was still unemployed. Then her partner was in a traffic accident and couldn't work for several months. Andrea confided to me that this dark time was the hardest of her life. It was easy to slip into hopelessness when they faced huge bills and wondered how to cut expenses even more. There were so many unknowns, so much waiting. Would this job application lead to a job? How much would insurance pay, and what kind of arrangements could they make to pay their bills over an extended period? Andrea said that it would all have been easier if they knew how long it would take for things to change, but they couldn't know that.

Unfortunately, some waiting times go on and on. In a crisis, we're energized and may have something immediate to do, but when the crisis becomes long term and chronic, energy begins to ebb and despair may overwhelm us. The challenge of living through darkness is to find something to hold on to as we wait. Andrea clung to hope and it brought her strength. What she discovered in herself was a determination to keep on trying that she didn't know she had, a strength that seemed to increase as she and her partner lived through this dark time.

Hope needs to be grounded in what is real and true. When it is, it can sustain and strengthen us in our dark waiting times. During the five years I visited my mother in a nursing home, she was wheelchair-bound and suffering from Alzheimer's disease. I couldn't hope for her recovery, but I did have hope. In the myriad small decisions I made, my desire was for her to have the best possible quality of life. I hoped that this day, this visit, would be a good one, that this time she would smile or laugh or maybe even sing old hymns with me. It was a dark waiting time, but joy and laughter were possible, too, and we found them together.

We need companions for waiting, but particularly for waiting in darkness. Discouragement and despair can assail us more swiftly when we are alone. Sometimes, being present with my mother's long diminishment was incredibly painful. After a visit when I held her hand as she writhed with back pain or desperately wanted to return to a husband and a home that were no longer there, I wept in despair. But I needed to weep with someone, to have someone with me in the painful darkness. My husband and a friend or two would sit with me, just as I sat with her.

Hope and companionship are treasures in darkness, strengthening us for the journey. An even greater treasure is God's love and companionship during this time. Trusting that God is with us in the darkness doesn't mean the darkness lifts. But we may experience the darkness differently. Often in darkness we can't feel God's presence, but we can still know it exists. It is especially helpful to have a friend affirm God's presence for us when we can't feel it, to hold the light of faith when ours flickers.

In the Psalms we repeatedly find reminders of times of darkness and testaments to God's enduring presence and help in them:

> I waited patiently for the Lord;
>   he inclined to me and heard my cry.
> He drew me up from the desolate pit,
>   out of the miry bog,
> And set my feet upon a rock,
>   making my steps secure.
>
> —Psalm 40:1–2

The prophet Jeremiah also carried God's message of comfort to a people in exile: "For surely I know the plans I have for you, says the Lord, plans for your welfare and not for harm, to give you a future with hope" (29:11). We, too, can take comfort from God's assurances of love: "I have loved you with an everlasting love; therefore I have continued my faithfulness to you" (Jeremiah 31:3). God's love is with us, no matter how dark the waiting is.

GOD IS ACTIVE HERE

The presence of God turns waiting times upside down, for waiting changes us, and God is in the changing. Waiting, in fact, can be the gift that matures us spiritually and readies us to move into the future. I discovered that sitting with my mother, holding her hand in shared silence, was a profoundly spiritual practice. It became my daily meditation, centering my day and teaching me to live with waiting.

Waiting time is sacred time. We can't fully see what is happening while we wait. Looking back at this time, we might understand it better. In the spiritual practice of walking a labyrinth, we follow an intricate path that circles around the center, sometimes drawing near and then moving farther away, but finally arriving at the center. Trusting that the labyrinth path eventually leads to the center is like trusting God during waiting times. Even when it seems as if we aren't getting any closer, something is happening.

This beautiful poem titled "Patient Trust," by Pierre Teilhard de Chardin, a philosopher, scientist, and Jesuit priest, teaches about trusting God in these waiting times. In the early 1900s his paleontological work led Teilhard to write about both the Creation and the Creator in ways that ran counter to Catholic teachings. As a result, his works were censured and denied publication during his lifetime. But today his book *The Phenomenon of Man* is a classic theological work, and his gentle encouragement to "trust in the slow work of God" continues to inspire us.

PATIENT TRUST

Above all, trust in the slow work of God.
We are quite naturally impatient in everything
	to reach the end without delay.
We should like to skip the intermediate stages.
We are impatient of being on the way to something
	unknown, something new.
And yet it is the law of all progress
	that it is made by passing through
	some stages of instability—
	and that it may take a very long time.

And so I think it is with you;
	your ideas mature gradually—let them grow,
	let them shape themselves, without undue haste.

Don't try to force them on,
	as though you could be today what time
	(that is to say, grace and circumstances
	acting on your own good will)
	will make of you tomorrow.

Only God could say what this new spirit
	gradually forming within you will be.
Give our Lord the benefit of believing
	that his hand is leading you,
and accept the anxiety of feeling yourself
	in suspense and incomplete.
						—Pierre Teilhard de Chardin

Practices for Finding Your Way

Practices in waiting times are twofold, deepening our awareness of waiting as a sacred space and supporting us while we wait, especially when we go through times of darkness. While these are individual practices, remember that the presence and support of other people is essential during our waiting times. Reach out to others.

BULBS IN WINTER

This meditation focuses on the gift at the heart of waiting by using the image of a sleeping bulb.

1. Find a quiet place where you will not be interrupted. Settle yourself in a comfortable position and notice your breathing, allowing it to quiet and calm you. Simply be present in the moment.
2. Imagine yourself settled deep in the earth as a bulb. Inside you rests all you will need to begin sending out that precious green shoot, but it is not yet time. Picture snow and cold winds above your snug nest, and take some time to be quietly resting and waiting. Accept this time; recognize that you need this cold in order to grow well, that this inactive time is a gift.
3. Return to your awareness of your human waiting time and reflect on the experience of being snugly protected in your waiting. How did you feel as a waiting bulb?
4. Reflect on any gifts you find in this present time of inactivity. How will you know when the waiting is over, when it is time to send out shoots?

HOLDING ON IN DARKNESS

Having something to hold on to through dark times can take many forms. This practice uses words, but you could also use a picture or a physical gesture or a piece of music that sustains and upholds you. It may be helpful to have something to hold on to from a religious tradition, such as prayer beads, or from the natural world, such as a shell or a stone.

1. Sitting quietly, acknowledge your present reality of waiting through a dark time. Do not lose yourself in it, but recognize that it is true.
2. Given that this time is dark, picture how you want to live through it. Find a few words that express that intention. Perhaps it will be *love, steadiness,* or *hope.* Try them on, saying to yourself "I choose ..."
3. You might also find the words you need in a few lines from poems or sacred writings. Fit one or two lines of the writing to accompany your breathing. As you breathe, repeat the words silently.
4. Repeat the words of intention or wisdom several times a day, especially when the waiting becomes particularly hard. You may also find new words with the power to support and sustain you.

BE STILL

Our human need to be actively doing something makes waiting times a particular challenge. This practice helps us release the stress of wishing to do something and being unable to.

1. Find a quiet place where you will not be interrupted. Settle comfortably and notice how you are sitting, choosing a posture in which your body can be relaxed. Be aware of your breathing, allowing it to be smooth and deep.
2. Notice any stress or tension you have in your body during this time of waiting. Where in your body are you carrying that tension?

3. Repeat silently to yourself a few words that express your desire to let go and be still. It may be a prayer offering this time to God. It may be a phrase that you fit into your breathing, something as simple as "Let go" or "I am here" or "Be still and know that I am God."

4. Be aware of your breathing, and let your body begin to release its tension. Begin to let go of any tightness and stress. Notice what areas of your body need this release, and deliberately relax them one at a time. With each breath out, let go and relax your body more.

5. Be in the waiting time with God. Breathe in this time of stillness, and stay within it as long as you can.

CHAPTER TEN

THE HARVEST OF DISCERNMENT

*The fruit of the Spirit is love, joy, peace, patience, kind-
ness, generosity, faithfulness, gentleness, and self-control.*
—*Galatians 5:22–23*

My husband and I have been friends with Linda and Sam for
many years. We've worked together, raised children together,
and shared neighborhoods, travel, and the deaths of our parents.
The other evening, when Sam posed the question "What makes
a successful life?" I wasn't surprised. He likes to throw out puz-
zlers like that. But I was surprised at how challenged we were by
the question. We're old enough to have experienced plenty of
successes, and plenty of failures, too.

Yet all of us were challenged by the word *success*. A successful life can be measured by many different criteria. Is it career
achievement, family happiness, financial prosperity? Is it winning
something your heart is set upon—anything from elected office to
land conservation to the league championship? The word *success*
indicates that what we did "worked," it was the "right choice,"
and it led to the successful life we wanted. It implies that *our*
efforts led to achievement in work, financial prosperity, family
happiness, or perhaps in following a drummer uniquely our own.

But judging our lives in those terms is far too limiting. So much beyond our own efforts shapes our lives. Perhaps a good job falls victim to a bad economy. A tragic accident takes the life of a loved one, and the suffering family falls apart. Success, however it is defined, can evade us despite our best intentions and efforts. Rejoicing in the achievement and success of a venture or grieving over its failure is not wrong, but using successful outcomes as a standard to measure our lives and our decisions is truly inadequate.

Spirit-led decision making doesn't guarantee a successful outcome, even though the practices of attentiveness we have been learning will bring wisdom to the process of deciding. However carefully we pay attention to the Spirit's promptings and follow the way that seems most right, other factors can sweep through, altering the landscape and changing the hoped-for outcome. What is certain is that the most important outcome of such spiritual discernment is a strong foundation for living. No matter what path our life takes—whether it is the one we've chosen or the one we've simply landed on—when our decisions are guided by the Spirit, we are strengthened in living it. In braiding together willingness, attentiveness, and responsiveness as a way of making decisions, we've created a rope to hold on to throughout all our days. That is the true harvest of a life of spiritual discernment.

Harvest rather than *success* is a better measure of spiritual decision making. What fruits of the harvest do we gather when we open ourselves to God, learn to pay attention, and learn to be responsive in making decisions? Whatever the shape of our daily lives, we receive a rich harvest that nurtures us and overflows into others' lives. It is not something to achieve or accomplish, not a place of arrival. It comes through the journey itself and from the intention we bring to the journey. It comes through faithfully following our desire to live in willingness, attentiveness, and responsiveness.

In my backyard garden is a bed of ever-bearing strawberries. Unlike the overwhelming but brief bounty of early summer strawberries, we enjoy these ever-bearing berries fresh from the patch or on top of desserts all summer long. The harvest of spiritual decision making is like that—it continues providing sweet fruit throughout our lives. There are many fruits of the Spirit. At the beginning of this chapter, Paul's letter to early Christians of Galatia includes an abundant list—love, joy, peace, patience, kindness, generosity, faithfulness, gentleness, and self-control—but the harvest is not limited to these. The specific gifts I describe below provide a sampling from the overflowing bounty of spiritual discernment fruits to enrich our lives.

THE FRUIT OF SEEING CLEARLY

In Richard Rohr's *Everything Belongs,* he describes Buddhism as "the religion of mirror-wiping." Buddhist practice, he says, is about "getting our ego-agenda out of the way, so *we can see things as they really are.*" Cleansing the lens is paying attention to who we really are—with love. When we open ourselves to Love, we see more clearly and understand more fully. We can look at ourselves with the help of a loving God and learn to accept what is true about ourselves, our stories, and our relationships with others.

The fruit of seeing clearly helps us see the truth of what is around us in the world. We shed illusion. We awaken more deeply to both beauty and to pain. We are more awake to injustice and need, and to the power of the human spirit to respond with love and compassion. Clear seeing is needed for major decision making and it helps us in our daily walk as well. It helps us really see the others on life's path with us.

I recently walked my young granddaughters down the street to the playground, a simple trip that was like a Buddhist practice of awareness for me. Because of them I saw things differently. I saw the tiny blue flower in the crack in the sidewalk and the way tree roots had heaved up the concrete paving. Through their slow walking, I noticed the people who passed, with their tired faces or their brisk intentness. I noticed the jauntiness of a young man moving to the music in his ear and the slow, steady pace of the old man with a cane in one hand and a leash for the poodle by his side in the other. Seeing them more clearly also made me wonder about their lives and their stories. Paying close attention to them destroyed the illusion that they were strangers totally separate from me and my life.

Seeing more clearly helps us to gain a clearer perspective on our place among people and in the world. At such times I remember that, no matter how pressing my need, I am not at the center of the world. Though Spirit-led decision making seems to focus on ourselves and our lives, it actually places us in truer relationship with the world around us. I am not the center of the mosaic or the only thread in the tapestry, but I am one among a multitude of beautiful tiles or shining threads. I have beauty and worth, and so do all the others.

Seeing myself clearly in relationship to other people with their own needs and journeys also brings another gift—the gift of humility. *Humility* means "of the earth," *humus*. We are all of the earth. Paradoxically, knowing this truth frees and enlarges us rather than diminishing us. With this awareness, we can live our common humanity more freely. We can simply be with what we know to be true, holding our unique piece of the mosaic in place among the other glowing tiles. It becomes easier to accept others as unique individuals with gifts and weaknesses, and ourselves in the same way.

THE FRUIT OF AUTHENTIC LIVING

Clear seeing opens us up to receive the fruit of authentic living. When we see more clearly what is real and true, we want to live that reality. We begin to live more from our true selves in relation to the people and the world around us. We are tasting the fruit of authentic living.

When Bonnie developed cancer, she faced a host of decisions, from treatments to work decisions to the kind of help she needed for daily life. At first, the crisis brought confusion, pain, and a feeling of being overwhelmed, but that was followed by a new sense of clarity and freedom. She began to see what was real and true—in herself and her situation—and that she could choose to live from the fruits of that seeing. She described it as "a strange mix of both speeding up and slowing down." She was "speeding up" because she felt more assertive and empowered to be true to herself in her speaking and living. While the old Bonnie would have hung back, silently accepting what others said, now she spoke up, asking for what she needed, whether it was medical information or someone to organize a system of meals to be delivered to her.

Bonnie also sensed a "slowing down." She began to feel the sacredness of each day in discerning how to live it. It gave her a clearer and stronger sense of *who* she was and *how* she was in relation to others. She no longer needed to struggle to prove her worth; she simply rested in being who she was. Knowing and accepting herself led her to feel greater peace about herself and her life than she had felt before the cancer. Stepping firmly and carefully through the journey of illness, she knew herself to be living more authentically each step of the way.

When we are rooted in what is real and true, we are living more deeply from our God-created selves; we're rooted in God's reality, God's truth. American theologian Howard Thurman used the word *genuine* to describe God's reality and truth when he wrote, "You must wait and listen for the sound of the genuine that is within you. When you hear it, that will be your voice and the Voice of God." When we hear the genuine, authentic voice, it is calling us to move into more authenticity in living, calling us to accept the gift of being grounded in God and freely growing into our true selves.

Authentic, genuine living brings a sense of inner freedom into our lives. Freedom means many things in our culture; we speak of the importance of political or religious freedom, freedom from want or from abusive relationships. At the heart of the longing for these freedoms lies the desire to be the person whom God has created us to be. As we live more authentically, hearing the "sound of the genuine," our freedom grows. Even if outer circumstances remain the same, the feeling of being free inside ourselves is nurtured as we learn to accept and honor our unique selves. Yes, we can say, this is my gift, my call, and my responsibility. No, we say, fear need not dominate; old labels, old hooks and attachments aren't limiting my path. I choose to live. The fruit of authentic living contains the seeds of authentic freedom for our lives.

THE FRUIT OF PEACE

A sense of peace is often considered a result of spiritual discernment. "Are you at peace with your decision?" someone may ask. Or perhaps you, with a quick internal survey, heave a sigh of gladness, and conclude, "Yes, this is right, I feel peaceful about it." On the other hand, a lingering unease is seen as a sign that things aren't quite right. When I met with Ellie, she summed it up by saying, "I must be clear about my decision. Otherwise I am *peace-less*." What does it mean to be *peace-less*? What does it mean to be *peace-full*?

When we think of peacefulness, we usually think of tranquility and serenity. To be peaceful is to be still and at ease, not driven, pressured, or in turmoil. Such peacefulness is indeed a rich and wonderful experience, although sometimes our lives appear more like oceans of confusion and turbulence dotted with brief islands of peacefulness. Certainly, opening to God and welcoming God's guidance doesn't guarantee a life filled with tranquility and calm. We still feel pulled in different directions, with many challenges along the way. And this happens, it seems, in spite of being willing to attend to the Guide.

And yet there is a kind of deep inner peace that can exist amid daily confusion and agitation. Like Brother Lawrence, a seventeenth-century Carmelite lay brother who "practiced the presence of God" in the middle of a bustling monastery kitchen, we can know peace even surrounded by the tumult of daily decisions. "If we wish to enjoy the peace of Paradise beginning in this life," Brother Lawrence wrote in a letter of advice, "we must become used to a familiar, humble, and loving conversation with God." In *Practicing the Presence of God,* the account of his life and spiritual wisdom, we discover that Brother Lawrence's peace was grounded in that ongoing companionship with God amid the bustle of a large monastery in an age of political upheaval.

The peace associated with feelings of serenity and tranquility can be disturbed by surface storms, while far below the surface, in the center of our being, there can still exist a place of peace, the place of "loving conversation with God." That deep-within-us peace is the fruit of our willingness to be open to God. It develops through our seeing clearly and making decisions for authentic living. We find an inner integrity in the acceptance of ourselves, our stories, and our carefully made decisions. We can stand within that deep peace as a place of central integration in our lives. Here I am, we can say, I am at peace with myself.

When Ellie spoke of being in turmoil, without peace, she was a single parent with two jobs, making a decision about money. The signs of peace she was looking for were deeper ones. She often felt caught between something she wanted for her young son and what she could afford. But this time she had done discernment homework, which included learning about budgeting and credit-card charges. She knew her spending limits and she knew that respecting them was important. An inner acceptance of what was real in her life and her decision to live with integrity within that reality brought her peace. Even though her son begged for the latest electronic gadget and she had to say "no," she had peace within herself. "Here I stand," she could say. "I am at peace."

The familiar quotation "God is not the author of confusion, but of peace" (1 Corinthians 14:33, KJV) reminds us of the deep inner core of peace that is the fruit of Spirit-led discernment. Such peace is like a deep, pure chime sounding in harmony with divine music, which may be clearly heard when we are attentive and listen for the harmony within ourselves.

THE FRUIT OF LOVE

In making decisions with the Spirit, we inevitably receive the fruit of love. God is love, and when we are willing, attentive, and responsive to God, we grow in love. We notice it around us, and we grow in giving and receiving it. Even when God is not named, the presence of love testifies to the presence of God.

When we are attentive to Love, we see more of God's presence around us. We see it in the tenderness of relationship between lovers, the listening and laughter between friends, the amazing patience in parents of small children, the welcome extended to one who lingers on the edge of the circle. When we're aware of Love, we notice God's presence in the smallest of details. On frosty nights while I sleep, my husband covers me with an additional blanket even though he's not cold. But he knows I chill easily, and he is saying "I love you" with this small act of loving-kindness.

When we notice Love's presence around us, it begins to shape our decisions. Then we, too, become the embodiment of God's love. Ed's story is an example of this. He needed to decide what to do about his difficult next-door neighbor. They shared a small backyard, and the neighbor's dog kept digging holes all over it, with a special interest in Ed's carefully tended flowerbeds. Ed and his neighbor had had previous exchanges about a blaring television, so Ed knew how quickly his neighbor could get angry.

When Ed opened the situation to God, willing to be attentive to whatever he might see, the first thing that he noticed was how important this dog was to his neighbor. His neighbor never seemed to go out with friends, and Ed wondered if the dog really *was* his neighbor's best friend. Ed decided that the first step would be to make friends with the man's dog. Then he would have a basis for talking more comfortably with his neighbor and he could speak of his concern for their yard.

Love was the fruit of Ed's discernment. As he gave love and attention to the dog (and received it, too!), he found a compassionate love growing in him for his neighbor. He saw more clearly who his neighbor was, not just the owner of this animal that was destroying his flowers, but a person who was somewhat shy and hid behind a gruff and angry exterior.

In paying attention to his neighbor, Ed's love showed itself through compassion and through forgiveness. Compassion is the love that feels another's distress and brokenness. Compassion does not eliminate our sense of judgment, but it enlarges our awareness so that we can understand others better and care for them as they are. We understand better how other people—our brothers and sisters—have experienced the world and how they are struggling.

Forgiveness—whether giving or receiving it—is a decision of love. We humans hurt each other in all kinds of ways. When we forgive, we are letting go because we love. It may be an act of love to one who hurt us, but it is also an act of love directed within to decide to release the hurt rather than clutch it to ourselves. Though we still see clearly the reality of the injury, we can choose to lay down the burden of resentment. Forgiveness is often a long, slow process of turning away from anger or bitterness, but the ability to forgive is a powerful gift of the God of love.

Love is a policy for living. As a part of the harvest of Spirit-led discernment, we receive love and decide to adopt the policy as our own.

THE FRUIT OF FULLNESS OF LIVING

Jesus calls this fruit *abundant* living, and describes his mission as offering an *abundant* life (John 10:10). To live in abundance could mean material abundance, but that is not what Jesus meant here. Jesus's teachings tend to awaken us to what is already present.

Paying attention awakens us to our lives and helps us appreciate more fully their depth and breadth. We awaken to much that we want to change, but we also awaken to the unexpected richness that already exists. Fullness of life is one of those truths. Abundance is already present if we can only see it and take it in. What would it mean to live, appreciating the fullness of the life we have? What would it be to live fully?

Some years ago I was invited to be the clerk of the Lancaster Quaker Meeting, to which I belonged. Since there is no paid staff, the clerk, who is part administrator and part discernment guide with a bit of pastor thrown in, takes on serious responsibility. I needed to carefully, prayerfully discern my response. What surprised me most was how the process of discernment itself changed me. I examined myself, my stage of life, my gifts and weaknesses, along with the community and its needs at that time. When I thought of my meeting community, I realized the treasure I already had. This group of people gave me a sense of home, and I felt committed to them. Before this I had taken my participation in the community for granted; now I woke up to the fullness of belonging there. I decided to say "yes" to the invitation. In the years that followed, I continued to grow spiritually and find my way as the community was finding its way. We journeyed together through seasons of struggle and seasons of great harmony, and I awakened more and more to the richness of the life we shared.

In the Jewish tradition, the greeting and farewell *Shalom aleichem* is usually translated as "Peace be with you." In many Muslim countries, a very similar phrase, *Salaam alaikum,* is used in the same way, as a greeting and blessing upon entering or leaving. But *shalom* or *salaam* means more than the English word *peace*; it is better translated as "wholeness," "completeness," and "fullness." What a marvelous greeting to extend to each other: Fullness of living be with you and yours!

Becoming whole or complete is like putting a jigsaw puzzle together. It begins as an impossible array of hundreds of small pieces, but as we work on it, we gradually see the picture taking shape. We see the beautiful Swiss chalet, surrounded by snow-covered peaks, promised by the picture on the box. All those pieces do make sense when they are fitted together. Examining our selves and our stories, testing our choices by taking steps one after the other, even waiting to see more clearly—all this helps us make sense of our own puzzle pieces, helps us create our own beautiful picture.

But discernment is different, for we never do *complete* our picture. Making decisions and putting pieces together is an ongoing process. As long as we are alive, we are engaged in becoming. With the Light to illuminate our way, fullness of living lies in *how* we live the rich incompleteness of our lives. It lies in how awake we are to our lifelong journey. The fruits of spiritual discernment are part of this unfolding journey. As these fruits flourish within us, we grow toward becoming peace, becoming love, toward clearer seeing and more authentic living. And the Spirit shows us the way.

Practices for Finding Your Way

These practices focus on acknowledging and welcoming the spiritual harvest found in decision making and discernment. They are also a reminder that the process, even more than the outcome, is central to spiritual living.

NAMING OF THE GIFTS

Taking each of the sections of this chapter as a guide, this practice deepens our awareness of the gifts of spiritual discernment. It is helpful to record your responses in a journal, since it is easy to take these gifts for granted and no longer notice them.

1. Find a quiet time and space for reflection on your process toward a specific decision. Take time to

remember the different stages of your decision making and how you have begun to take steps into living what you have decided.

2. Turn to one of the five sections on the fruits of discernment in this chapter and read through it again. Consider its place in your life, particularly asking yourself how you have grown in this area through being willing, attentive, and responsive. For example: How have you lived in a way that is more authentic and true to yourself? How have you experienced love? Remember, we don't constantly experience these fruits of the spirit. Perhaps you will notice only small examples, but include them, too.

3. Consider other fruits of this Spirit-led decision-making process in addition to the ones highlighted in this chapter. The biblical quotation at the beginning of the chapter is a good place to start, but look beyond that, too. How have you changed and grown through opening to the Spirit, through becoming more attentive, through taking steps or waiting?

4. Having listed all you can at this time, offer a prayer of gratitude for this harvest. Return to this practice in the future to remember, be grateful, and add to the list.

THE BODY WELCOMES THE GIFTS

Through this practice, your body welcomes the gifts of the Spirit and expresses a sense of becoming a channel through which these gifts can flow. This is a good practice to follow the previous one.

1. Sit or stand comfortably and notice your breathing. Notice its rise and fall, allowing it to calm and center you.

2. Name a specific fruit of Spirit-led discernment, and reach your arms and hands upward to receive the gift.

Then turn your hands inward to your heart to embrace and accept the gift. Finally, in a movement showing your willingness to spread the blessing of this gift among others, turn your arms and hands outward to the world. Allow your movements to be slow and prayerful, feeling each step as your body enacts it.

3. Repeat the process, naming other fruits of the Spirit. Pause between each repetition until your body is ready to welcome another gift. You could be aware of the gift of clarity or a more loving heart or moments of deep inner peace with your journey. What other gifts would you name?

DREAM FOR TOMORROW

This practice looks at how you have changed through this process of spiritual discernment and imagines who you may grow into becoming. Imagining can strengthen you for living into this dream for tomorrow.

1. Sitting comfortably in a quiet place, simply notice your steady breathing for a while. Your breaths may deepen and lengthen as you sit quietly and relax.

2. Recognize that the process of spiritual decision making has changed you and is continuing to change you. Be aware of who you are now and how the fruits of this process have changed you.

3. Imagine yourself continuing to grow in the days and months to come. Picture the person you would like to be and take the time to see yourself growing into being that person. See yourself being in large and small ways the kind of person you and God dream of you being.

4. As you continue to relax, return to the day immediately before you and picture yourself entering it. Invite God to be with you this day and in all future days.

A LETTER FOR
DECISION MAKERS

In chapter 8, I wrote about Chris, who had lost his job in fundraising and saw this as an opportunity to follow his dream of developing a theater company. He was caught between his passion for developing his dream and his need to generate income for himself and his family.

Recently, I saw Chris again. Joined by his wife Tabea, we looked together at their ongoing decision making. I was aware of how carefully and faithfully they were moving through their decision-making process—striving to be open and willing, to pay attention, to respond with small trial steps, and then returning to their willingness and attentiveness. They are very much in the middle, unsure of where their path will take them. This letter is for them, and for you, too, as you make your way through your decisions—those you face today and those that await you in the future.

~o

Dear friends,
First of all, please take time to be still. The psalmist wrote, "Be still, and know that I am God" (46:10). In our urgency to find a way forward, ideas, questions, answers,

and unknowns often swirl around us so quickly that we have little time for stillness, little time to pause. I believe there are truths you already know about what you can have and do in this season of your life. You need time to be still enough to recognize them. These truths are deeper than the immediate decisions facing you. The next step in your decision will become clearer after you acknowledge the deeper truths. Stop jumping around. Be still and listen for what you already know.

In the stillness, I hope you will come to feel God's presence in your decision making. I believe we are all in a "God story," a story of our lives being shaped through God's presence and through our attentiveness to God's presence. You, as much as Abraham and Sarah, are in a God story. Recognizing that truth changes things. It helps you think about decisions differently and provides a foundation for your decision making. You are a co-creator with God of the unique God story you are living. Attentive to divine wisdom, you participate in building the story.

Trust the story you are in. The shape for it has been created by the commitments you have made and by your present stage of life. These realities create a particular vessel in which you can flourish, although vessels have inherent limitations as well. There may be options that are not open to you at this time. Trust that there is also great freedom to grow within this stage of your story and that it will nurture what is to come next.

It is hard to trust the story when you can't see clearly. There are so many unknowns, and any step you may decide to take can feel risky. You may look back and say, "I wish I had made another decision. This didn't work out as I had hoped." You may take on your dream with enthusiasm, but discover that it's impossible to make a living with it or that you can't give it the time it demands.

Recognizing that we're in a God story never means that everything turns out perfectly. What it does mean is that we continue to thoughtfully and prayerfully discern the way forward from where we are. And it means that we can trust that all the decisions of our lives, even those we might come to see as mistakes or false starts, bring gifts to strengthen and teach us for the next stage of the journey—if we allow them.

One of the gifts of a time of intense decision making is heightened awareness. We often journey along barely noticing where we are because the road is so familiar. Suddenly something happens and we wake up. We don't know where we are anymore! We begin to pay attention. Right now in the middle of decision making, you are awake and paying attention. Treasure this gift. Even when the road becomes familiar, keep noticing what is around you and within you. Be awake to the daily freshness of the familiar. Give yourself the gift of awe and amazement.

Children often ask, "Are we there yet?" when they are traveling. We adults sometimes ask the same question, "Have we gotten there yet? Have we arrived?" when we think of our unfolding lives and all our decisions. Unfortunately, thinking that we *have* arrived, that we have everything settled and are finished with change, handicaps us in making decisions for the future. The truth is that our God stories go on as long as we live, and so does our decision making.

I imagine God's reply to my "Are we there yet?" It goes something like this: "No, child, but take my hand and come along. We have more decisions to make, more of the story to create. Let's be on our way."

Nancy

A Six-Session Course of Study and Practice

This book encourages readers to think about themselves and their lives, to make life-changing decisions, and to grow spiritually through self-understanding and opening to God. That's a tall order! Having companions along the way makes the process easier.

While anyone can read and follow this process independently, the benefit of a group lies in the support and encouragement participants give each other. Members can rejoice and commiserate together. They can share experiences and offer insight and wisdom to each other. They can hold each other accountable to continue the journey of spiritual growth and decision making.

HOW TO FORM YOUR GROUP

If you are interested in working through the process outlined in this book, you can invite a few friends to join you for regular sessions. If you are part of a religious organization, you might contact the appropriate committee to extend an invitation to participate to the whole community. While the focus is on making decisions, participants do not need to be involved in major life decisions to benefit from a group that uses this book.

If you want to have a companion, but an organized group isn't possible, you could simply ask one other person to join you in the reading and practices described here. Two or three can support, encourage, and provide accountability for each other just as a larger group can.

OUTLINE FOR EACH SESSION

The sessions are designed to be an hour and a half to two hours long. As participants grow closer to each other, the sessions may get longer.

> **Opening:** 5–15 minutes. Having a ritual to open (and close) each session indicates the beginning of a different way of being together after the initial socializing as the group gathers. This can be a chime, a simple chant or song, or the lighting of a candle. A reading is suggested for each session.
>
> **Group Discussion:** 30 minutes. This is a time for general discussion and responding to the material in the assigned chapters. Possible discussion questions are included.
>
> **Break:** 10–15 minutes.
>
> **Time for Sharing and Support:** 30 minutes. In smaller groups of three to five, each participant speaks of his or her own process of decision making and spiritual discernment and receives support and encouragement from the others. Possible areas for sharing are listed for each session.
>
> **Closing:** 5–15 minutes. As in the opening, a ritual can be helpful. Readings are suggested for each session, but being silently prayerful together can also provide a good closing ritual.

ADVICE FOR GROUPS

1. This guide contains six sessions. The experience is best when they are not weekly sessions. Monthly or biweekly gatherings will give a fuller opportunity to read the assigned chapters, reflect on the reading, and do the practices. With more time, there is more space to develop deepened

understanding about yourself and to grow into the decisions you are working on.

2. Each session needs a designated facilitator. It may be one person, or the leadership can rotate among the participants. The responsibility of the facilitator is to open and close the gathering, and, keeping track of the time, to guide the group from one part of the session to the next.

3. Participants should make a commitment to attend regularly. The trust that grows as people share and support each other through change is undermined when group members don't show up faithfully.

4. Group members honor each others' stories by listening with respect to what is shared, not by giving outright advice or initiating problem solving, unless the speaker explicitly requests it. No one knows the full story of another's life, and the best gift we can give one another is to listen.

5. It is essential to hold in confidence what is said in the group.

6. All group members need a journal or notebook in which to keep their reflections about what has been learned and their experiences in the practices.

7. No matter how rich the group experience, the most important part is done by participants on their own. All members need to participate through reading, doing practices, and reflecting on the self-understanding and decisions that unfold through the six sessions. Depending on life situations, there may be a sizable range in how much each person does, but everyone needs to be engaged with the process outside of the group gatherings.

8. Adapt the ideas and structure of the following sessions so that they will best fit your group.

～◌

SESSION ONE: MAKING A START

BEFORE SESSION ONE

Read the introduction, "Making a Start" (and more, if you wish). Choose a journal or notebook that will be dedicated to this experience.

OPENING

The leader gathers the group with a welcome and an opening ritual.

Begin with a prayer or a reading. An appropriate reading is from Isaiah 43:19:

> I am about to do a new thing;
> > now it springs forth, do you not perceive it?
> I will make a way in the wilderness
> > and rivers in the desert.

Since this is the first gathering, go around the circle and introduce yourselves by sharing your name and what drew you to participate in the group. Then confirm the organization and expectations of your group.

SUGGESTED DISCUSSION QUESTIONS

Consider the three strands that we braid together as we make decisions with God. Are there other words you would use instead of *willingness, attentiveness,* and *responsiveness*? Which of the three themes is strongest in your decision making? Which is hardest for you?

Can you recall a "survival decision" you've made, such as those the author describes in "Making a Start"? What about a "fulfillment decision"?

Are there any "decision clusters" that you can identify in your life—small decisions that cluster around a strong value you hold?

BREAK

TIME FOR SHARING AND SUPPORT

Larger groups should divide up so there are only three to five people together. This is a time for each person to speak and to listen to each other.

As you begin this journey, what do you want to discover about yourself?

Are there specific decisions that you are facing? If so, what are the various aspects of the decision, the factors that make it challenging?

CLOSING

The leader reads Hafiz's "It Felt Love" (see page 15). In a moment of silence, picture yourself opening and trusting in the loving environment of this group.

SESSION TWO: BEING WILLING

BEFORE SESSION TWO

Read chapters 1 and 2, and do some or all of the practices. Journal about your response to the readings and your experiences with the practices.

OPENING

The leader opens with a prayer, a reading, or music. A possible reading is Isaiah 43:1–2,4 (from the "Accepting Love" practice in chapter 2).

SUGGESTED DISCUSSION QUESTIONS

How would you describe an attitude of being willing? What is the difference between willingness and willfulness? What are signs of willingness and willfulness?

Which of the fears that the author describes do you think are usually most powerful? Why are they powerful?

BREAK

TIME FOR SHARING AND SUPPORT

Larger groups form small groups of three to five, with each participant sharing from his or her own experience.

What experiences have you had with the practices of these last few weeks? What have you learned or found helpful? What has been difficult or really challenging for you?

To what questions in your life have you responded with a wholehearted "yes"? How has that "yes" shaped you? Have there been many times you said "maybe"? How have those times of sitting on the fence shaped your life?

If you come with the intention of making a decision or changing in some way, tell the group about it. What kind of support do you need?

CLOSING

The leader reads the opening meditation on willingness on page 12. Allow a brief silence for reflection.

SESSION THREE: PAYING ATTENTION

BEFORE SESSION THREE

Read chapters 3 and 4 and do at least two practices from each chapter. These practices are rich, so give yourself as much time as you can. Especially important are "The Circle Story" (chapter 3) and "Two Ideal Days" (chapter 4). Continue journaling about your experiences.

OPENING

The leader opens with a prayer, a reading, or music. This reading from Anthony de Mello's *The Way to Love* could be used:

> Everywhere in the world people are in search of love, for everyone is convinced that love alone can save the world, love alone can make life meaningful and worth living.
>
> The first act of love is to see this person or this object, this reality as it truly is ... otherwise it is not the person you love but the idea you have formed about this person.
>
> The second ingredient is equally important ... to see yourself, to ruthlessly flash the light of awareness on your motives, your emotions, your needs. This means calling things by their name.... If you achieve this kind of awareness of the other and yourself, you will know what love is.

SUGGESTED DISCUSSION QUESTIONS

What ways of paying attention or listening suggested in chapters 3 and 4 are new to you?

What gives power to the things in our lives that hook us or to which we are attached? How can you distinguish between a healthy closeness and an unhealthy attachment?

When faced with a decision to be made quickly, a person's initial response tends to be either a feeling or a thinking response. Which is your typical first response? What kinds of decision making bring forth a feeling response? What kinds of decision making call forth a thinking response?

Break

Time for Sharing and Support

In small groups, participants speak of their own experience and listen with love to the others while considering these questions.

Which practices did you do during the last few weeks and what did you learn from them? What did you find challenging or difficult? What has helped you understand yourself better?

Share a dream or a passion with the group. No matter how far-fetched it seems, say it out loud.

If you are working on making a decision, what have you learned about yourself and the situation that can help you gain greater clarity about your decision?

Closing

The leader reminds the group that the focus for the next session is chapters 5 and 7. Chapter 6 will be covered in the last session. The session closes by reading the opening meditation on attentiveness on page 46. Allow a brief silence for reflection.

Session Four: A Pause to Listen and Reflect

Before Session Four

Read chapters 5 and 7, and do practices from them. Continue to journal about what you learn and the challenges you find. The *"Examen* for God's Invitations" (chapter 5), "Looking at the Themes," and "Travel Each Path" (both chapter 7) are particularly recommended practices.

Opening

The leader opens with a prayer, a reading, or music. The reading could be the following poem from Kent Ira Groff's *Facing East, Praying West:*

Choosing Well, Living Whole

Sometimes choosing is like
a ship going straight to port:
no hesitation or negotiation:
the heart's Desire is clear.

Sometimes choosing is like
sailing with an untoward wind
the pulls of consolations,
the counter-pulls of desolations.
But, Ah! You tack into the stress;
with skill you follow your bliss.

Other times there's no movement.
You're dead in the water: you yearn
for disturbance or assurance yet
get only deafening echoes of apathy.

Then is when you take the challenge
to chart an inner course to change:
gather information—facts and feelings;
picture the choice in your mind's eye,
then weigh its pros and cons.

Imagine a colleague in your shoes,
what do you say to help the person choose?
Imagine yourself at the end of life:
what choice gives inward peace, less strife?
With Gandhi, picture the poorest person
in the world—then make your decision.

Present your Self wholly to God:
How does this choice sit
with your head, your heart,
and the pattern of your faith journey?

—Kent Ira Groff

Suggested Discussion Questions

Chapter 7 opens with a quotation from Thomas Kelly's *Testament of Devotion*. Reread it, and consider whether it applies to you and your life. Who are some members of your committee of selves? Is anyone in charge?

The author emphasizes that noticing God's nudges is something we can do better if we quiet ourselves. What helps you to quiet yourself so you can be attentive?

Egos need to proclaim themselves, and be recognized and accepted by others. Self-identity is an interior sense of self that isn't based on other people's opinions or acknowledgments. Do you agree with this explanation of the difference between ego and self-identity?

Break

Time of Sharing and Support

In small groups, participants speak from their own experience and listen with love and encouragement to the others.

Which practices did you do and what did you learn? What did you find challenging or difficult?

In chapter 7, the author names cultural standards for decision making and alternative standards. Which standards are most important to your decisions? Which standards influence you more than you would like? Are there some that you wish were more important in your decision making?

Over the last few weeks, what has helped you better understand yourself and the choices you are making or will be making?

Are you growing closer to a decision? What steps are you ready to take? Which steps might you take in the next month?

CLOSING

The leader closes with these words from Esther de Waal's *Lost in Wonder*, allowing a brief time of silence at the end.

> I long for fullness of life and it is frightening to think that I might be wasting that most precious of God's gifts, the chance to live fully and freely. Stopping to take time to look at the pattern of my life, and to think and pray about it, will almost inevitably mean that I not only learn more about God but I discover more about myself.

SESSION FIVE: TIME FOR STEPPING OUT AND TIME FOR WAITING

BEFORE SESSION FIVE

Read chapters 8 and 9, and do practices from them. Continue to journal about your readings and experiences. For those actively taking steps in decision making, the practice "Two Steps a Week" is particularly recommended.

OPENING

The leader opens the session with a prayer, a reading, or music. A suggested reading is the opening meditation on responsiveness on page 112.

SUGGESTED DISCUSSION QUESTIONS

The author says there is always a step to be taken. She suggests that our "step" may even be how we respond to times of waiting. Do you agree with her? Have there been times when you felt there was nothing to be done?

Have you experienced the difference between "waiting for" and "waiting while" that the author describes? What was happening in the waiting time?

Have you found trail angels along your path? What did they look like and what gift did they bring you?

BREAK

TIME FOR SHARING AND SUPPORT

In small groups, participants speak of their own experiences and listen with love and encouragement to the others.

Which practices did you do and what did you learn? What did you find challenging or difficult? Are there practices from the earlier chapters that are becoming a habit for you, a regular part of your life?

How have you stepped forward? This may be an exploratory "testing the waters" step or a clear decision you are beginning to act on. If you have not made any changes, what do you think is holding you back?

CLOSING

The leader closes the group session with a reading of "Patient Trust" by Pierre Teilhard de Chardin (see page 157).

SESSION SIX: DISCERNMENT AS A WAY OF LIFE

BEFORE SESSION SIX

Read chapters 6 and 10. Choose practices to engage with. Chapter 6 contains practices that may become part of your everyday routine, so try a variety of them and begin to build them into your daily life. In chapter 10, "Naming of the Gifts" is particularly recommended.

OPENING

The leader opens with a prayer, a reading, or a song. The following reflection from the writings of Julian of Norwich, a fourteenth-century English mystic could be used.

He showed me a little thing, the size of a hazelnut, in the palm of my hand, and it was as round as a ball. I looked at it with my mind's eye and I thought, "What can this be?" And answer came, "It is all that is made." I marveled that it could last, for I thought it might have crumbled to nothing, it was so small. And the answer came into my mind, "It lasts and ever shall because God loves it." And all things have being through the love of God.

In this little thing I saw three truths. The first is that God made it. The second is that God loves it. The third is that God looks after it.

What is he indeed that is maker and lover and keeper? I cannot find words to tell. For until I am one with him I can never have true rest nor peace. I can never know it until I am held so close to him that there is nothing in between.

—*Daily Readings with Julian*
of Norwich, Volume 1

SUGGESTED DISCUSSION QUESTIONS

As this is the final gathering, there could be a wide-ranging discussion covering the whole journey. Specific discussion questions addressing the readings of this session might include the following:

In chapter 6, spiritual habits of attentiveness in daily life are emphasized. What has been particularly valuable in your life? Are there any that you'd like to develop in your own life?

Do you agree with the author that there will be a harvest of the spiritual discernment process, no matter what the outcome of a particular decision?

BREAK

TIME FOR SHARING AND SUPPORT

Participants speak of their experiences and listen with love and encouragement to the others.

What uncertainties or grieving do you experience as you come to the closing of this group journey?

What invitation do you feel for further decisions and life change?

What trail angels have you found within the group? You may wish to name specific examples of receiving support, encouragement, or being held accountable.

CLOSING AND CELEBRATION

It is good to have a ritual of closing and celebration that is special and unique for those of you who have traveled together. Allow extra time for this. Encourage each group member to contribute in some way. Here are two possibilities.

Each person might light a candle from a central candle and speak briefly. Perhaps each person names an experience or area of focus that was a particular gift of this time spent together. The gift might simply be a word or a phrase used during the sessions, or a few lines from the book that were particularly meaningful.

Each person takes a turn as the focus of the group. Others in the group can offer brief thanks or blessings for that person and her journey.

SUGGESTIONS FOR FURTHER READING

ON SPIRITUAL DISCERNMENT AND DECISION MAKING

Au, Wilkie, and Noreen Cannon Au. *The Discerning Heart: Exploring the Christian Path*. Mahwah, N.J.: Paulist Press, 2006.

Bill, J. Brent. *Sacred Compass: The Way of Spiritual Discernment*. Brewster, Mass.: Paraclete Press, 2008.

Dougherty, Rose Mary. *Discernment: A Path to Spiritual Awakening*. Mahwah, N.J.: Paulist Press, 2009.

Farnham, Suzanne, Joseph P. Gill, R. Taylor McLean, and Susan M. Ward. *Listening Hearts: Discerning Call in Community*. Harrisburg, Pa.: Morehouse, 1991.

Flanagan, Eileen. *The Wisdom to Know the Difference: When to Make a Change—and When to Let Go*. New York: Tarcher, 2009.

Isenhower, Valerie K., and Judith A. Todd. *Living into the Answers: A Workbook for Personal Spiritual Discernment*. Nashville, Tenn.: Upper Room Books, 2008.

Loring, Patricia. *Spiritual Discernment: The Context and Goal of Clearness Committees*. Wallingford, Pa.: Pendle Hill, 1992.

Palmer, Parker J. *Let Your Life Speak: Listening for the Voice of Vocation*. San Francisco: Jossey-Bass, 2000.

Rohr, Richard, and Andreas Ebert. *Discovering the Enneagram: An Ancient Tool for a New Spiritual Journey*. New York: Crossroad, 1991.

Silf, Margaret. *Inner Compass: An Invitation to Ignatian Spirituality*. Chicago: Loyola Press, 1999.

MORE GUIDANCE FOR THE SPIRITUAL JOURNEY

De Mello, Anthony. *The Way to Love: The Last Meditations of Anthony de Mello*. New York: Doubleday, 1992.

De Waal, Esther. *Lost in Wonder: Rediscovering the Spiritual Art of Attentiveness*. Collegeville, Minn.: Liturgical Press, 2003.

Edwards, Tilden. *Living in the Presence: Spiritual Exercises to Open Our Lives to the Awareness of God*. New York: HarperCollins, 1995.

Gruen, Anselm. *Heaven Begins Within You: Wisdom from the Desert Fathers*. Translated by Peter Heinegg. New York: Crossroad, 1999.

Guenther, Margaret. *At Home in the World: A Rule of Life for the Rest of Us*. New York: Seabury Books, 2006.

Kelly, Thomas R. *A Testament of Devotion*. New York: HarperCollins, 1969.

Kidd, Sue Monk. *When the Heart Waits: Spiritual Direction for Life's Sacred Questions*. San Francisco: HarperCollins, 1990.

Lawrence of the Resurrection. *Practicing the Presence of God*. Brewster, Mass.: Paraclete Press, 2007.

Lindahl, Kay. *Practicing the Sacred Art of Listening: A Guide to Enrich Your Relationships and Kindle Your Spiritual Life*. Woodstock, Vt.: SkyLight Paths, 2003.

———. *The Sacred Art of Listening: Forty Reflections for Cultivating a Spiritual Practice*. Woodstock, Vt.: SkyLight Paths, 2002.

Loring, Patricia. *Listening Spirituality: Personal Spiritual Practices Among Friends*. Washington Grove, Md.: Openings Press, 1997.

May, Gerald G. *The Awakened Heart: Opening Yourself to the Love You Need*. San Francisco: HarperCollins, 1991.

———. *Will and Spirit: A Contemplative Psychology*. San Francisco: HarperSanFrancisco, 1982.

Merton, Thomas. *Thomas Merton: Essential Writings*. Edited by Christine M. Bochen. Maryknoll, N.Y.: Orbis Books, 2000.

———. *A Thomas Merton Reader*. Edited by Thomas P. McDonnell. New York: Image, 1974.

Muller, Wayne. *Sabbath: Finding Rest, Renewal, and Delight in Our Busy Lives*. New York: Bantam, 1999.

Nhat Hanh, Thich. *Living Buddha, Living Christ*. New York: Riverhead Books, 1995.

———. *The Miracle of Mindfulness: A Manual on Meditation*. Rev. ed. Boston: Beacon Press, 1987.

Nouwen, Henri J. M. *The Inner Voice of Love: A Journey Through Anguish to Freedom*. New York: Doubleday, 1998.

Rohr, Richard. *Everything Belongs: The Gift of Contemplative Prayer*. Rev. ed. New York: Crossroad, 2003.

Shapiro, Rami. *The Sacred Art of Lovingkindness: Preparing to Practice.* Woodstock, Vt.: SkyLight Paths, 2006.

Steindl-Rast, David. *Gratefulness, the Heart of Prayer: An Approach to Life in Fullness.* New York: Paulist Press, 1984.

Taylor, Barbara Brown. *An Altar in the World: A Geography of Faith.* New York: HarperCollins, 2009.

Thurston, Bonnie. *To Everything a Season: A Spirituality of Time.* New York: Crossroad, 1999.

Weil, Simone. *Waiting for God.* New York: Harper Perennial Modern Classics, 2009.

Whitmire, Catherine. *Plain Living: A Quaker Path to Simplicity.* Notre Dame, Ind.: Sorin Books, 2001.

Wuellner, Flora Slosson. *Prayer and Our Bodies.* Nashville, Tenn.: Upper Room Books, 1987.

OTHER WORKS CITED

Buber, Martin. *Tales of the Hasidim.* Translated by Olga Marx. New York: Schocken, 1975.

Buechner, Frederick. *Wishful Thinking: A Theological ABC.* New York: Harper & Row, 1973.

Fox, Caroline. *Memories of Old Friends: Being Extracts from the Journals and Letters of Caroline Fox, of Penjerrick, Cornwall, from 1835 to 1871.* 1882. Reprint, n.p.: Nabu Press, 2010.

Groff, Kent Ira. *Facing East, Praying West: Poetic Reflections on the Spiritual Exercises.* Mahwah, N.J.: Paulist Press, 2010.

Hafiz. *The Gift: Poems by Hafiz, the Great Sufi Master.* Translated by Daniel Ladinsky. New York: Penguin Compass, 1999.

Hammarskjold, Dag. *Markings.* New York: Vintage, 2006.

Julian of Norwich. *Daily Readings with Julian of Norwich.* Edited by Robert Llewelyn. Vol. 1. Springfield, Ill.: Templegate, 1986.

Lamott, Anne. *Traveling Mercies: Some Thoughts on Faith.* New York: Pantheon, 1999.

Lewis, C. S. *The Silver Chair.* New York: HarperCollins, 1981.

Penn, William. *Some Fruits of Solitude: Wise Sayings on the Conduct of Human Life.* Edited by Eric K. Taylor. Scottdale, Pa.: Herald Press, 2003.

Roth, Gabrielle. *Maps to Ecstasy: A Healing Journey for the Untamed Spirit.* Novato, Calif.: Nataraj, 1998.

Woolman, John. *The Journal and Major Essays of John Woolman.* Edited by Phillips P. Moulton. Richmond, Ind.: Friends United Press, 1989.

ACKNOWLEDGMENTS

A book is never the product of only one person's inspiration and work. I am very grateful to all those who have contributed to this book becoming a reality. I am grateful to SkyLight Paths Publishing, which guided the progress of this project, and to Marcia Broucek, whose phone call asking me if I'd ever considered writing about spiritual discernment started the project rolling.

I am thankful for supportive friends who asked about the work and listened lovingly to my sometimes long-winded recounting of my writing adventures during this past year. I have special thank-yous to Tom Gates, Glenn Mitchell, Marc Oehler, Melissa Stock, and Roland Stock, who gave their time to read through the manuscript as it was being shaped.

My deepest gratitude is to my husband, Larry Bieber, and my daughters, Alisa Bieber and Diana Bieber Locke, who not only listened lovingly to me and read the manuscript (with many valuable editing suggestions!) but rearranged their own lives to give me time to work. I love you and I thank you.

Finally I am grateful for the blessing of all those who shared their stories with me through my years of listening. Any wisdom in this book comes from your lives as much as mine. The rich mine of life experiences I have drawn from in the writing is a gift from all of you.

INDEX OF EXERCISES

Inspiration

Finding Time for the Timeless: Spirituality in the Workweek
By John McQuiston II
Offers refreshing stories of everyday spiritual practices people use to free themselves from the work and worry mindset of our culture.
5⅛ x 6½, 208 pp, Quality PB, 978-1-59473-383-3 **$9.99**

God the What?: What Our Metaphors for God Reveal about Our Beliefs in God by Carolyn Jane Bohler
Inspires you to consider a wide range of images of God in order to refine how you imagine God. 6 x 9, 192 pp, Quality PB, 978-1-59473-251-5 **$16.99**

How Did I Get to Be 70 When I'm 35 Inside?: Spiritual Surprises of Later Life by Linda Douty
Encourages you to focus on the inner changes of aging to help you greet your later years as the grand adventure they can be. 6 x 9, 208 pp, Quality PB, 978-1-59473-297-3 **$16.99**

Restoring Life's Missing Pieces: The Spiritual Power of Remembering & Reuniting with People, Places, Things & Self by Caren Goldman
A powerful and thought-provoking look at reunions of all kinds as roads to remembering and re-membering ourselves.
6 x 9, 208 pp, Quality PB, 978-1-59473-295-9 **$16.99**

Saving Civility: 52 Ways to Tame Rude, Crude & Attitude for a Polite Planet
By Sara Hacala
Provides fifty-two practical ways you can reverse the course of incivility and make the world a more enriching, pleasant place to live.
6 x 9, 240 pp, Quality PB 978-1-59473-314-7 **$16.99**

Spiritually Healthy Divorce: Navigating Disruption with Insight & Hope
by Carolyne Call
A spiritual map to help you move through the twists and turns of divorce.
6 x 9, 224 pp, Quality PB, 978-1-59473-288-1 **$16.99**

Who Is My God? 2nd Edition
An Innovative Guide to Finding Your Spiritual Identity
by the Editors at SkyLight Paths
Provides the Spiritual Identity Self-Test™ to uncover the components of your unique spirituality. 6 x 9, 160 pp, Quality PB, 978-1-59473-014-6 **$15.99**

Journeys of Simplicity
Traveling Light with Thomas Merton, Bashō,
Edward Abbey, Annie Dillard & Others
by Philip Harnden
Invites you to consider a more graceful way of traveling through life.
PB includes journal pages to help you get started on
your own spiritual journey.
5 x 7¼, 144 pp, Quality PB, 978-1-59473-181-5 **$12.99**
5 x 7¼, 128 pp, HC, 978-1-893361-76-8 **$16.95**

Or phone, mail or e-mail to: SKYLIGHT PATHS Publishing
An imprint of Turner Publishing Company
4507 Charlotte Avenue • Suite 100 • Nashville, Tennessee
Tel: (615) 255-2665• www.skylightpaths.com
Prices subject to change.

Sacred Texts—SkyLight Illuminations Series

Offers today's spiritual seeker an enjoyable entry into the great classic texts of the world's spiritual traditions. Each classic is presented in an accessible translation, with facing pages of guided commentary from experts, giving you the keys you need to understand the history, context and meaning of the text.

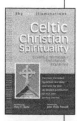

CHRISTIANITY

Celtic Christian Spirituality: Essential Writings—Annotated & Explained
Annotation by Mary C. Earle; Foreword by John Philip Newell
Explores how the writings of this lively tradition embody the gospel.
5½ x 8½, 176 pp, Quality PB, 978-1-59473-302-4 **$16.99**

Desert Fathers and Mothers: Early Christian Wisdom Sayings—Annotated & Explained
Annotation by Christine Valters Paintner, PhD
Opens up wisdom of the desert fathers and mothers for readers with no previous knowledge of Western monasticism and early Christianity.
5½ x 8½, 192 pp, Quality PB, 978-1-59473-373-4 **$16.99**

The End of Days: Essential Selections from Apocalyptic Texts—Annotated & Explained
Annotation by Robert G. Clouse, PhD
Helps you understand the complex Christian visions of the end of the world.
5½ x 8½, 224 pp, Quality PB, 978-1-59473-170-9 **$16.99**

The Hidden Gospel of Matthew: Annotated & Explained
Translation & Annotation by Ron Miller
Discover the words and events that have the strongest connection to the historical Jesus.
5½ x 8½, 272 pp, Quality PB, 978-1-59473-038-2 **$16.99**

The Infancy Gospels of Jesus: Apocryphal Tales from the Childhoods of Mary and Jesus—Annotated & Explained
Translation & Annotation by Stevan Davies; Foreword by A. Edward Siecienski, PhD
A startling presentation of the early lives of Mary, Jesus and other biblical figures that will amuse and surprise you.
5½ x 8½, 176 pp, Quality PB, 978-1-59473-258-4 **$16.99**

John & Charles Wesley: Selections from Their Writings and Hymns—Annotated & Explained
Annotation by Paul W. Chilcote, PhD
A unique presentation of the writings of these two inspiring brothers brings together some of the most essential material from their large corpus of work.
5½ x 8½, 288 pp, Quality PB, 978-1-59473-309-3 **$16.99**

The Lost Sayings of Jesus: Teachings from Ancient Christian, Jewish, Gnostic and Islamic Sources—Annotated & Explained
Translation & Annotation by Andrew Phillip Smith; Foreword by Stephan A. Hoeller
This collection of more than three hundred sayings depicts Jesus as a Wisdom teacher who speaks to people of all faiths as a mystic and spiritual master.
5½ x 8½, 240 pp, Quality PB, 978-1-59473-172-3 **$16.99**

Philokalia: The Eastern Christian Spiritual Texts—Selections
Annotated & Explained *Annotation by Allyne Smith; Translation by G. E. H. Palmer, Phillip Sherrard and Bishop Kallistos Ware*
The first approachable introduction to the wisdom of the Philokalia, the classic text of Eastern Christian spirituality.
5½ x 8½, 240 pp, Quality PB, 978-1-59473-103-7 **$16.99**

The Sacred Writings of Paul: Selections Annotated & Explained
Translation & Annotation by Ron Miller
Leads you into the exciting immediacy of Paul's teachings.
5½ x 8½, 224 pp, Quality PB, 978-1-59473-213-3 **$16.99**

Prayer / Meditation

Sacred Attention: A Spiritual Practice for Finding God in the Moment
by Margaret D. McGee
Framed on the Christian liturgical year, this inspiring guide explores ways to develop a practice of attention as a means of talking—and listening—to God.
6 x 9, 144 pp, Quality PB, 978-1-59473-291-1 **$16.99**

Women Pray: Voices through the Ages, from Many Faiths, Cultures and Traditions
Edited and with Introductions by Monica Furlong
5 x 7¼, 256 pp, Quality PB, 978-1-59473-071-9 **$15.99**

Women of Color Pray: Voices of Strength, Faith, Healing, Hope and Courage
Edited and with Introductions by Christal M. Jackson
Through these prayers, poetry, lyrics, meditations and affirmations, you will share in the strong and undeniable connection women of color share with God.
5 x 7¼, 208 pp, Quality PB, 978-1-59473-077-1 **$15.99**

Secrets of Prayer: A Multifaith Guide to Creating Personal Prayer in Your Life   *by Nancy Corcoran, CSJ*
This compelling, multifaith guidebook offers you companionship and encouragement on the journey to a healthy prayer life. 6 x 9, 160 pp, Quality PB, 978-1-59473-215-7 **$16.99**

Prayers to an Evolutionary God
by William Cleary; Afterword by Diarmuid O'Murchu
Inspired by the spiritual and scientific teachings of Diarmuid O'Murchu and Teilhard de Chardin, reveals that religion and science can be combined to create an expanding view of the universe—an evolutionary faith.
6 x 9, 208 pp, HC, 978-1-59473-006-1 **$21.99**

The Art of Public Prayer, 2nd Edition: Not for Clergy Only
by Lawrence A. Hoffman, PhD 6 x 9, 288 pp, Quality PB, 978-1-893361-06-5 **$19.99**

A Heart of Stillness: A Complete Guide to Learning the Art of Meditation
by David A. Cooper 5½ x 8½, 272 pp, Quality PB, 978-1-893361-03-4 **$18.99**

Meditation without Gurus: A Guide to the Heart of Practice
by Clark Strand 5½ x 8½, 192 pp, Quality PB, 978-1-893361-93-5 **$16.95**

Praying with Our Hands: 21 Practices of Embodied Prayer from the World's Spiritual Traditions   *by Jon M. Sweeney; Photos by Jennifer J. Wilson; Foreword by Mother Tessa Bielecki; Afterword by Taitetsu Unno, PhD*
8 x 8, 96 pp, 22 duotone photos, Quality PB, 978-1-893361-16-4 **$16.95**

Three Gates to Meditation Practice: A Personal Journey into Sufism, Buddhism, and Judaism   *by David A. Cooper* 5½ x 8½, 240 pp, Quality PB, 978-1-893361-22-5 **$16.95**

Prayer / M. Basil Pennington, OCSO

Finding Grace at the Center, 3rd Edition: The Beginning of Centering Prayer   *with Thomas Keating, OCSO, and Thomas E. Clarke, SJ; Foreword by Rev. Cynthia Bourgeault, PhD* A practical guide to a simple and beautiful form of meditative prayer. 5 x 7¼, 128 pp, Quality PB, 978-1-59473-182-2 **$12.99**

The Monks of Mount Athos: A Western Monk's Extraordinary Spiritual Journey on Eastern Holy Ground   *Foreword by Archimandrite Dionysios*
Explores the landscape, monastic communities and food of Athos.
6 x 9, 352 pp, Quality PB, 978-1-893361-78-2 **$18.95**

Psalms: A Spiritual Commentary   *Illus. by Phillip Ratner*
Reflections on some of the most beloved passages from the Bible's most widely read book. 6 x 9, 176 pp, 24 full-page b/w illus., Quality PB, 978-1-59473-234-8 **$16.99**

The Song of Songs: A Spiritual Commentary   *Illus. by Phillip Ratner*
Explore the Bible's most challenging mystical text.
6 x 9, 160 pp, 14 full-page b/w illus., Quality PB, 978-1-59473-235-5 **$16.99**
HC, 978-1-59473-004-7 **$19.99**

Women's Interest

Women, Spirituality and Transformative Leadership
Where Grace Meets Power
Edited by Kathe Schaaf, Kay Lindahl, Kathleen S. Hurty, PhD, and Reverend Guo Cheen
A dynamic conversation on the power of women's spiritual leadership and its emerging patterns of transformation. 6 x 9, 288 pp, Hardcover, 978-1-59473-313-0 **$24.99**

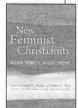

Spiritually Healthy Divorce: Navigating Disruption with Insight & Hope
by Carolyne Call A spiritual map to help you move through the twists and turns of divorce. 6 x 9, 224 pp, Quality PB, 978-1-59473-288-1 **$16.99**

New Feminist Christianity: Many Voices, Many Views
Edited by Mary E. Hunt and Diann L. Neu
Insights from ministers and theologians, activists and leaders, artists and liturgists who are shaping the future. Taken together, their voices offer a starting point for building new models of religious life and worship.
6 x 9, 384 pp, HC, 978-1-59473-285-0 **$24.99**

New Jewish Feminism: Probing the Past, Forging the Future
Edited by Rabbi Elyse Goldstein; Foreword by Anita Diamant
Looks at the growth and accomplishments of Jewish feminism and what they mean for Jewish women today and tomorrow. Features the voices of women from every area of Jewish life, addressing the important issues that concern Jewish women.
6 x 9, 480 pp, Quality PB, 978-1-58023-448-1 **$19.99**; HC, 978-1-58023-359-0 **$24.99***

Bread, Body, Spirit: Finding the Sacred in Food
Edited and with Introductions by Alice Peck 6 x 9, 224 pp, Quality PB, 978-1-59473-242-3 **$19.99**

Dance—The Sacred Art: The Joy of Movement as a Spiritual Practice
by Cynthia Winton-Henry 5½ x 8½, 224 pp, Quality PB, 978-1-59473-268-3 **$16.99**

Daughters of the Desert: Stories of Remarkable Women from Christian, Jewish and Muslim Traditions
by Claire Rudolf Murphy, Meghan Nuttall Sayres, Mary Cronk Farrell, Sarah Conover and Betsy Wharton
5½ x 8½, 192 pp, Illus., Quality PB, 978-1-59473-106-8 **$14.99** Inc. reader's discussion guide

The Divine Feminine in Biblical Wisdom Literature
Selections Annotated & Explained
Translation & Annotation by Rabbi Rami Shapiro; Foreword by Rev. Cynthia Bourgeault, PhD
5½ x 8½, 240 pp, Quality PB, 978-1-59473-109-9 **$16.99**

Divining the Body: Reclaim the Holiness of Your Physical Self
by Jan Phillips 8 x 8, 256 pp, Quality PB, 978-1-59473-080-1 **$18.99**

Honoring Motherhood: Prayers, Ceremonies & Blessings
Edited and with Introductions by Lynn L. Caruso
5 x 7¼, 272 pp, Quality PB, 978-1-58473-384-0 **$9.99**; HC, 978-1-59473-239-3 **$19.99**

Next to Godliness: Finding the Sacred in Housekeeping
Edited by Alice Peck 6 x 9, 224 pp, Quality PB, 978-1-59473-214-0 **$19.99**

ReVisions: Seeing Torah through a Feminist Lens
by Rabbi Elyse Goldstein 5½ x 8½, 224 pp, Quality PB, 978-1-58023-117-6 **$16.95***

The Triumph of Eve & Other Subversive Bible Tales
by Matt Biers-Ariel 5½ x 8½, 192 pp, Quality PB, 978-1-59473-176-1 **$14.99**

White Fire: A Portrait of Women Spiritual Leaders in America
by Malka Drucker; Photos by Gay Block 7 x 10, 320 pp, b/w photos, HC, 978-1-893361-64-5 **$24.95**

Woman Spirit Awakening in Nature: Growing Into the Fullness of Who You Are
by Nancy Barrett Chickerneo, PhD; Foreword by Eileen Fisher
8 x 8, 224 pp, b/w illus., Quality PB, 978-1-59473-250-8 **$16.99**

Women of Color Pray: Voices of Strength, Faith, Healing, Hope and Courage
Edited and with Introductions by Christal M. Jackson
5 x 7¼, 208 pp, Quality PB, 978-1-59473-077-1 **$15.99**

The Women's Torah Commentary: New Insights from Women Rabbis on the 54 Weekly Torah Portions *Edited by Rabbi Elyse Goldstein*
6 x 9, 496 pp, Quality PB, 978-1-58023-370-5 **$19.99**; HC, 978-1-58023-076-6 **$34.95***

* A book from Jewish Lights, SkyLight Paths' sister imprint

Spirituality

Gathering at God's Table: The Meaning of Mission in the Feast of Faith
By Katharine Jefferts Schori
A profound reminder of our role in the larger frame of God's dream for a restored and reconciled world. 6 x 9, 256 pp, HC, 978-1-59473-316-1 **$21.99**

The Heartbeat of God: Finding the Sacred in the Middle of Everything
by Katharine Jefferts Schori; Foreword by Joan Chittister, OSB
Explores our connections to other people, to other nations and with the environment through the lens of faith. 6 x 9, 240 pp, HC, 978-1-59473-292-8 **$21.99**

A Dangerous Dozen: Twelve Christians Who Threatened the Status Quo but Taught Us to Live Like Jesus
by the Rev. Canon C. K. Robertson, PhD; Foreword by Archbishop Desmond Tutu
Profiles twelve visionary men and women who challenged society and showed the world a different way of living. 6 x 9, 208 pp, Quality PB, 978-1-59473-298-0 **$16.99**

Decision Making & Spiritual Discernment: The Sacred Art of Finding Your Way *by Nancy L. Bieber*
Presents three essential aspects of Spirit-led decision making: willingness, attentiveness and responsiveness. 5½ x 8½, 208 pp, Quality PB, 978-1-59473-289-8 **$16.99**

Laugh Your Way to Grace: Reclaiming the Spiritual Power of Humor
by Rev. Susan Sparks A powerful, humorous case for laughter as a spiritual, healing path. 6 x 9, 176 pp, Quality PB, 978-1-59473-280-5 **$16.99**

Bread, Body, Spirit: Finding the Sacred in Food
Edited and with Introductions by Alice Peck 6 x 9, 224 pp, Quality PB, 978-1-59473-242-3 **$19.99**

Claiming Earth as Common Ground: The Ecological Crisis through the Lens of Faith
by Andrea Cohen-Kiener; Foreword by Rev. Sally Bingham
6 x 9, 192 pp, Quality PB, 978-1-59473-261-4 **$16.99**

Creating a Spiritual Retirement: A Guide to the Unseen Possibilities in Our Lives
by Molly Srode 6 x 9, 208 pp, b/w photos, Quality PB, 978-1-59473-050-4 **$14.99**

Creative Aging: Rethinking Retirement and Non-Retirement in a Changing World
by Marjory Zoet Bankson 6 x 9, 160 pp, Quality PB, 978-1-59473-281-2 **$16.99**

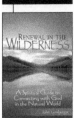

Keeping Spiritual Balance as We Grow Older: More than 65 Creative Ways to Use Purpose, Prayer, and the Power of Spirit to Build a Meaningful Retirement
by Molly and Bernie Srode 8 x 8, 224 pp, Quality PB, 978-1-59473-042-9 **$16.99**

Hearing the Call across Traditions: Readings on Faith and Service
Edited by Adam Davis; Foreword by Eboo Patel
6 x 9, 352 pp, Quality PB, 978-1-59473-303-1 **$18.99**; HC, 978-1-59473-264-5 **$29.99**

Honoring Motherhood: Prayers, Ceremonies & Blessings
Edited and with Introductions by Lynn L. Caruso
5 x 7¼, 272 pp, Quality PB, 978-1-58473-384-0 **$9.99**; HC, 978-1-59473-239-3 **$19.99**

The Losses of Our Lives: The Sacred Gifts of Renewal in Everyday Loss
by Dr. Nancy Copeland-Payton 6 x 9, 192 pp, HC, 978-1-59473-271-3 **$19.99**

Renewal in the Wilderness: A Spiritual Guide to Connecting with God in the Natural World *by John Lionberger*
6 x 9, 176 pp, b/w photos, Quality PB, 978-1-59473-219-5 **$16.99**

Soul Fire: Accessing Your Creativity
by Thomas Ryan, CSP 6 x 9, 160 pp, Quality PB, 978-1-59473-243-0 **$16.99**

A Spirituality for Brokenness: Discovering Your Deepest Self in Difficult Times
by Terry Taylor 6 x 9, 176 pp, Quality PB, 978-1-59473-229-4 **$16.99**

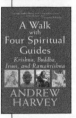

A Walk with Four Spiritual Guides: Krishna, Buddha, Jesus, and Ramakrishna
by Andrew Harvey 5½ x 8½, 192 pp, b/w photos & illus., Quality PB, 978-1-59473-138-9 **$15.99**

The Workplace and Spirituality: New Perspectives on Research and Practice
Edited by Dr. Joan Marques, Dr. Satinder Dhiman and Dr. Richard King
6 x 9, 256 pp, HC, 978-1-59473-260-7 **$29.99**

Spiritual Practice

Laugh Your Way to Grace: Reclaiming the Spiritual Power of Humor
by Rev. Susan Sparks A powerful, humorous case for laughter as a spiritual, healing path. 6 x 9, 176 pp, Quality PB, 978-1-59473-280-5 **$16.99**

Haiku—The Sacred Art: A Spiritual Practice in Three Lines
by Margaret D. McGee Introduces haiku as a simple and effective way of tapping into the sacred moments that permeate everyday living.
5½ x 8½, 192 pp, Quality PB, 978-1-59473-269-0 **$16.99**

Dance—The Sacred Art: The Joy of Movement as a Spiritual Practice
by Cynthia Winton-Henry Invites all of us, regardless of experience, into the possibility of dance/movement as a spiritual practice.
5½ x 8½, 224 pp, Quality PB, 978-1-59473-268-3 **$16.99**

Spiritual Adventures in the Snow: Skiing & Snowboarding as Renewal for Your Soul *by Dr. Marcia McFee and Rev. Karen Foster; Foreword by Paul Arthur* Explores snow sports as tangible experiences of the spiritual essence of our bodies and the earth. 5½ x 8½, 208 pp, Quality PB, 978-1-59473-270-6 **$16.99**

Divining the Body: Reclaim the Holiness of Your Physical Self *by Jan Phillips*
8 x 8, 256 pp, Quality PB, 978-1-59473-080-1 **$16.99**

Everyday Herbs in Spiritual Life: A Guide to Many Practices
by Michael J. Caduto; Foreword by Rosemary Gladstar
7 x 9, 208 pp, 20+ b/w illus., Quality PB, 978-1-59473-174-7 **$16.99**

The Gospel of Thomas: A Guidebook for Spiritual Practice
by Ron Miller; Translations by Stevan Davies 6 x 9, 160 pp, Quality PB, 978-1-59473-047-4 **$14.99**

Hospitality—The Sacred Art: Discovering the Hidden Spiritual Power of Invitation and Welcome *by Rev. Nanette Sawyer; Foreword by Rev. Dirk Ficca*
5½ x 8½, 208 pp, Quality PB, 978-1-59473-228-7 **$16.99**

Labyrinths from the Outside In: Walking to Spiritual Insight—A Beginner's Guide *by Donna Schaper and Carole Ann Camp*
6 x 9, 208 pp, b/w illus. and photos, Quality PB, 978-1-893361-18-8 **$16.95**

Practicing the Sacred Art of Listening: A Guide to Enrich Your Relationships and Kindle Your Spiritual Life *by Kay Lindahl* 8 x 8, 176 pp, Quality PB, 978-1-893361-85-0 **$16.95**

Recovery—The Sacred Art: The Twelve Steps as Spiritual Practice *by Rami Shapiro; Foreword by Joan Borysenko, PhD* 5½ x 8½, 240 pp, Quality PB, 978-1-59473-259-1 **$16.99**

Running—The Sacred Art: Preparing to Practice *by Dr. Warren A. Kay; Foreword by Kristin Armstrong* 5½ x 8½, 160 pp, Quality PB, 978-1-59473-227-0 **$16.99**

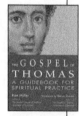

The Sacred Art of Bowing: Preparing to Practice
by Andi Young 5½ x 8½, 128 pp, b/w illus., Quality PB, 978-1-893361-82-9 **$14.95**

The Sacred Art of Chant: Preparing to Practice
by Ana Hernández 5½ x 8½, 192 pp, Quality PB, 978-1-59473-036-8 **$15.99**

The Sacred Art of Fasting: Preparing to Practice
by Thomas Ryan, CSP 5½ x 8½, 192 pp, Quality PB, 978-1-59473-078-8 **$15.99**

The Sacred Art of Forgiveness: Forgiving Ourselves and Others through God's Grace
by Marcia Ford 8 x 8, 176 pp, Quality PB, 978-1-59473-175-4 **$16.99**

The Sacred Art of Listening: Forty Reflections for Cultivating a Spiritual Practice
by Kay Lindahl; Illus. by Amy Schnapper 8 x 8, 160 pp, b/w illus., Quality PB, 978-1-893361-44-7 **$16.99**

The Sacred Art of Lovingkindness: Preparing to Practice
by Rabbi Rami Shapiro; Foreword by Marcia Ford 5½ x 8½, 176 pp, Quality PB, 978-1-59473-151-8 **$16.99**

Sacred Attention: A Spiritual Practice for Finding God in the Moment
by Margaret D. McGee 6 x 9, 144 pp, Quality PB, 978-1-59473-291-1 **$16.99**

Sacred Speech: A Practical Guide for Keeping Spirit in Your Speech
by Rev. Donna Schaper 6 x 9, 176 pp, Quality PB, 978-1-59473-068-9 **$15.99**
HC, 978-1-893361-74-4 **$21.95**

Soul Fire: Accessing Your Creativity
by Thomas Ryan, CSP 6 x 9, 160 pp, Quality PB, 978-1-59473-243-0 **$16.99**

Thanking & Blessing—The Sacred Art: Spiritual Vitality through Gratefulness
by Jay Marshall, PhD; Foreword by Philip Gulley 5½ x 8½, 176 pp, Quality PB, 978-1-59473-231-7 **$16.99**

About SKYLIGHT PATHS Publishing

SkyLight Paths Publishing is creating a place where people of different spiritual traditions come together for challenge and inspiration, a place where we can help each other understand the mystery that lies at the heart of our existence.

Through spirituality, our religious beliefs are increasingly becoming a part of our lives—rather than *apart* from our lives. While many of us may be more interested than ever in spiritual growth, we may be less firmly planted in traditional religion. Yet, we do want to deepen our relationship to the sacred, to learn from our own as well as from other faith traditions, and to practice in new ways.

SkyLight Paths sees both believers and seekers as a community that increasingly transcends traditional boundaries of religion and denomination—people wanting to learn from each other, *walking together, finding the way.*

For your information and convenience, at the back of this book we have provided a list of other SkyLight Paths books you might find interesting and useful. They cover the following subjects:

Buddhism / Zen	Global Spiritual	Monasticism
Catholicism	Perspectives	Mysticism
Children's Books	Gnosticism	Poetry
Christianity	Hinduism /	Prayer
Comparative	Vedanta	Religious Etiquette
Religion	Inspiration	Retirement
Current Events	Islam / Sufism	Spiritual Biography
Earth-Based	Judaism	Spiritual Direction
Spirituality	Kabbalah	Spirituality
Enneagram	Meditation	Women's Interest
	Midrash Fiction	Worship

Or phone, mail or e-mail to: SKYLIGHT PATHS Publishing
An imprint of Turner Publishing Company
4507 Charlotte Avenue • Suite 100 • Nashville, Tennessee
Tel: (615) 255-2665• www.skylightpaths.com
Prices subject to change.

For more information about each book,
visit our website at www.skylightpaths.com